I0408295

STAFF WHITE PAPER ON
ANTI-MARKET MANIPULATION ENFORCEMENT EFFORTS
TEN YEARS AFTER EPACT 2005

Federal Energy Regulatory Commission
November 2016

Staff White Paper on Anti-Market Manipulation Enforcement Efforts Ten Years After EPAct 2005

Staff White Paper on
Anti-Market Manipulation Enforcement Efforts Ten Years After EPAct 2005

I. Introduction

Market manipulation threatens the integrity of energy markets. It does so by its actual consequences—harming consumers, rendering prices and price-setting mechanisms inaccurate and unreliable, interfering with market operations, siphoning money away from market participants who are playing by the rules, and other ills that should have no place in our nation's energy markets. It also does so by causing entities participating in, benefiting from, or affected by energy markets to lose confidence that markets are working fairly and producing results consistent with market rules and fundamentals. This became starkly and dramatically clear during the Western Energy Crisis of 2000–2001, when Enron and other companies engaged in a variety of manipulative schemes that wreaked havoc on energy markets that were designed to ensure optimal rates for energy market participants and consumers based on economic principles of supply and demand. The schemes, which have been well documented,[1] were sophisticated, wide-ranging, and reflected major structural changes that had taken place in energy markets over the past three decades. The existence of these schemes, and the inability of government to effectively detect, stop, and penalize them, were—and remain—wholly incompatible with well-functioning energy markets that are essential to our society.

Since the 1980s, the Commission has transitioned from a cost-based, rate-setting function to oversight of a market regime designed to deliver energy at competitive prices. Along with its benefits, this transition has led to markets that are increasingly complex, with features such as physical and financial derivative products, new market operators in Independent System Operators (ISOs) and Regional Transmission Organizations (RTOs) administering complex market rules and products, electronic trading tools and platforms, and a host of new market participants besides the traditional public utilities. This increased complexity, in turn, has resulted in, and will continue to result in, sophisticated market participants looking for new ways to profit from market transactions—both lawfully but in some cases through manipulative schemes.

---

[1] *See, e.g., Am. Elec. Power Serv. Corp.*, 103 FERC ¶ 61,345, at PP 37–60 (2003), *reh'g denied*, 106 FERC ¶ 61,020 (2004) (*Gaming Order*); *San Diego Gas & Elec. Co. v. Sellers of Energy & Ancillary Servs.*, 149 FERC ¶ 61,116 (2014); FERC, *Final Report on Price Manipulation in Western Markets: Fact-Finding Investigation of Potential Manipulation of Electric and Natural Gas Prices*, Docket No. PA02-2-000 (Mar. 26, 2003) (*Final Report on Price Manipulation in Western Markets*).

During the Western Energy Crisis, the Commission's enforcement tools lagged behind these market developments, and the schemes exposed a major weakness in the Commission's ability to fulfill its core mission of ensuring just and reasonable rates and protect energy market participants and consumers. Until the Commission enacted the Market Behavior Rules applicable to electric markets and code of conduct applicable to natural gas markets in the aftermath of the Western Energy Crisis,[2] neither the statutes administered by the Commission nor its rules, regulations, or orders contained any explicit prohibition or definition of market manipulation. And in any event, the Commission lacked adequate civil penalty authority to effectively deter and sanction market manipulation,[3] and lacked tools to effectively oversee and surveil potentially problematic conduct occurring in jurisdictional energy markets.

The Commission's weak enforcement tools, combined with the breadth and creativity of the manipulative schemes during the Western Energy Crisis, prompted Congress to augment the Commission's existing authorities with a new broad authority to prohibit market manipulation, as well as enhanced penalty authority to meaningfully enforce the new law, in the Energy Policy Act of 2005 (EPAct 2005).[4] In passing the new law, Congress was clear in directing the Commission to take a powerful and resilient

---

[2] *See Investigation of Terms and Conditions of Public Utility Market-Based Rate Authorizations*, 105 FERC ¶ 61,218 (2003); *Amendments to Blanket Sales Certificate*, 105 FERC ¶ 61,217 (2003). The Commission enacted these rules pursuant to its authority to ensure just and reasonable rates.

[3] At the time, the Commission could assess penalties of only $11,000 per day under Part 1 and sections 210-214 of Part 2 of the Federal Power Act (FPA) and $5,550 per day under the Natural Gas Policy Act of 1978 (NGPA). 16 U.S.C. §§ 823b(c), 825o-1 (2000); 15 U.S.C. § 3414(b)(6) (2000); 18 C.F.R. § 385.1602 (2016). It lacked civil penalty authority for violations of section 205 of the FPA, requiring rates, terms, and conditions to be just and reasonable and not unduly discriminatory or preferential. The Commission also lacked civil penalty authority entirely under the Natural Gas Act (NGA). As former FERC Commissioner (and later Chairman) Joseph Kelliher stated in 2005: "This lack of civil penalty authority is a severe handicap in the Commission's enforcement of market rules." Joseph T. Kelliher, *Market Manipulation, Market Power, and the Authority of the Federal Energy Regulatory Commission*, 26 ENERGY L.J. 1, at 23 (2005). The Commission's principal remedial tool at the time was its authority to issue refunds. *See* 16 U.S.C. § 824e(b) (2012).

[4] Pub. L. No. 109-58, 119 Stat. 594 (2005); 16 U.S.C. § 824v(a) (2012) ("Prohibition of Energy Market Manipulation" under FPA); 16 U.S.C. § 825o-1 (2012) (penalty authority of $1,000,000 per day per violation under the FPA); 15 U.S.C. § 717c-1 (2012) ("Prohibition on Market Manipulation" under NGA); 15 U.S.C. § 717t-1 (2012) (penalty authority of $1,000,000 per day per violation under the NGA).

stand against market manipulation. For example, at one of the many Enron-related congressional hearings, a Senate Committee member told the Commission's then-Chairman, Patrick Wood III:

> I hope that we are able to look back at your tenure, Mr. Wood, and say that you dramatically changed it, you had an emergency [brake], you had aggressive overseers, you were an aggressive regulator, you saw wrongdoing, and that you took action immediately. I hope that is the legacy you will leave at that agency.[5]

The Commission promptly implemented the law, adopting its Anti-Manipulation Rule in Order No. 670 in January 2006.[6] This new rule, which reflected the expansive statutory language, gave the Commission broad authority to keep up with the evolving nature of complex energy markets and schemes occurring in those markets.[7]

Staff now has more than ten years of experience investigating and pursuing enforcement actions under the Anti-Manipulation Rule. During this time, staff has investigated more than 100 manipulation-related matters and continues to examine potential manipulation in numerous pending investigations. It has settled twenty-four

---

[5] *Examining Enron: Developments Regarding Electricity Price Manipulation in California: Hearing Before the Subcomm. on Consumer Affairs, Foreign Commerce and Tourism of the S. Comm. on Commerce, Science, and Transportation,* 107th Cong. 135 (2002) (Examining Enron) (Statement of Sen. Byron Dorgan, Chairman, Subcommittee on Consumer Affairs, Foreign Commerce and Tourism); *see also id.* at 144 (statement of Sen. Byron Dorgan to Patrick Wood III, Chairman, Federal Energy Regulatory Commission) ("[B]e a tiger."); *California Energy Markets: Refunds and Reform: Hearing Before the Subcomm. on Energy Policy, Natural Resources and Regulatory Affairs of the H. Comm. on Gov't Reform,* 108th Cong. 38 (2003) (Statement of Rep. Doug Ose, Chairman, Subcommittee on Energy Policy, Natural Resources and Government Affairs) (directing the Commission to send a "clear and unequivocal message about this kind of behavior not being tolerated").

[6] *Prohibition of Energy Market Manipulation,* Order No. 670, FERC Stats. & Regs. ¶ 31,202, *reh'g denied,* 114 FERC ¶ 61,300 (2006) (Order No. 670); *see also* 18 C.F.R. Part 1c (2016).

[7] In the aftermath of the Western Energy Crisis, the Commission also dedicated more resources and staff to detect and sanction market manipulation. For example, in 2002, it strengthened its oversight function by creating the Office of Market Oversight and Investigation, the predecessor to the current Office of Enforcement. *See* Examining Enron at 107. Also, in 2012, it created the Division of Analytics and Surveillance within the Office of Enforcement to enhance its surveillance capabilities and provide analysis and other assistance with market manipulation-related investigations.

manipulation-related investigations, tried two in administrative proceedings, and currently has six pending in United States district courts on petitions to affirm Commission orders assessing civil penalties.[8] In addition, staff has closed many of its market manipulation investigations without further action. Along the way, the Commission and courts have developed a body of law that, while still in its early stages and continuing to evolve, identifies and provides notice on specific types of conduct that can constitute market manipulation in the energy markets and factors that are indicative of such conduct. In addition, the Commission has identified relevant factors that can mitigate or aggravate the culpability and sanctions for such conduct. Equally important, staff has gained experience determining which factors lead us to close market manipulation matters without action.

Consistent with our efforts during the past ten years to conduct our enforcement program in a transparent and fair manner, staff issues this White Paper to provide insight on these lessons learned. Specifically, this White Paper provides information on: (1) some of the various factors that have been found to be indicative of fraudulent conduct under the Anti-Manipulation Rule; (2) some of the specific types of conduct and behaviors that have been found to constitute market manipulation; (3) mitigating and aggravating factors that have lessened or heightened an entity's culpability and sanctions for such conduct; and (4) the types of cases that staff has closed without action and the various factors that led to such decisions.[9] This White Paper is being issued simultaneously with a White Paper on Effective Energy Trading Compliance Practices.[10]

---

[8] Appendix A provides a complete list of these Commission-approved settlements, administrative proceedings, and pending district court petitions. In addition to the investigations listed, staff has undertaken far more inquiries to determine whether to open a market manipulation investigation.

[9] While this White Paper provides some examples and indicia of manipulative conduct, they are not meant to be exhaustive lists and avoidance of the conduct described here will not necessarily shield an entity from, or provide a defense to, an enforcement action. Staff and the Commission will consider all the facts and circumstances of a case in determining whether a violation occurred. In addition, while staff aims to provide guidance in numerous forms, such as its Annual Reports on Enforcement, presentations at industry conferences, and this White Paper, the ultimate and best guidance comes directly from Commission orders, such as orders approving settlement agreements, Orders to Show Cause, Orders Assessing Civil Penalties, and relevant court decisions.

[10] *See* Office of Enforcement White Paper on Effective Energy Trading Compliance Practices (Nov. 17, 2016) (Compliance Practices White Paper). The Compliance Practices White Paper is available on the Commission's website.

II. Background

Under the FPA and NGA, the Commission's core responsibility has been to ensure just and reasonable rates for transmission or sale of electric energy and transportation or sale of natural gas at wholesale in interstate commerce.[11] That core responsibility has been unaltered by subsequent regulatory changes that set rates for jurisdictional sales through market mechanisms rather than through cost-of-service ratemaking.[12]

To address manipulative practices employed during the Western Energy Crisis, the Commission created a set of Market Behavior Rules for electric sellers with market-based rate authority, as well as a new code of conduct for natural gas sellers with blanket certificates.[13] These new rules included blanket prohibitions on market manipulation in the electric and natural gas markets.[14] These rules provided notice to sellers of conduct that would be prohibited in all jurisdictional markets, and provided the Commission with clear authority to take action against sellers who engaged in such manipulative conduct.[15]

---

[11] 16 U.S.C. §§ 824, 824d (2012); 15 U.S.C. § 717c (2012).

[12] *See Calif. ex rel. Lockyer v. FERC*, 383 F.3d 1006, 1014-1016 (9th Cir. 2004) (affirming the Commission's authority to rely on market mechanisms to set just and reasonable rates, but only coupled with "implied enforcement mechanisms" sufficient to address the sorts of manipulative trading strategies employed during the Western Energy Crisis that would have pushed rates outside the zone of reasonableness); *Investigation of Terms and Conditions of Public Utility Market-Based Rate Authorizations*, 97 FERC ¶ 61,220, 61,976 (2001) ("We have a responsibility under the FPA to monitor wholesale markets to ensure that jurisdictional rates in the markets remain within a zone of reasonableness. Our responsibility is to ensure that sellers not charge unjust and unreasonable wholesale rates, and that the market structures and market rules governing public utility sellers nationwide, and affecting the wholesale rates of such public utility sellers, do not result in, or have the potential to result in, wholesale rates that are unjust, unreasonable, unduly discriminatory, or preferential.").

[13] *Investigation of Terms and Conditions of Public Utility Market-Based Rate Authorizations*, 105 FERC ¶ 61,218; *Amendments to Blanket Sales Certificate*, 105 FERC ¶ 61,217.

[14] *Investigation of Terms and Conditions of Public Utility Market-Based Rate Authorizations*, 105 FERC ¶ 61,218 at P 35 (adopting Market Behavior Rule 2, which prohibited "Actions or transactions that are without a legitimate business purpose and that are intended to or foreseeably could manipulate market prices, market conditions, or market rules for electric energy or electricity products"); *Amendments to Blanket Sales Certificate*, 105 FERC ¶ 61,217 at P 27 (adopting same prohibition in natural gas markets).

[15] When the Commission took action against sellers who had engaged in manipulative "gaming" practices in California's markets during the Western Energy

However, the Commission's authority to take meaningful enforcement action against entities who engaged in manipulation was still somewhat limited: the prohibition was applicable only to electric sellers with market-based rate authority and natural gas sellers with blanket certificates, and while the Commission could revoke such authorities and certificates, and had the power to direct disgorgement of unjust profits, it lacked authority to impose significant civil penalties under the FPA and lacked civil penalty authority altogether under the NGA.[16]

Congress addressed these limitations in EPAct 2005. That legislation provided for significant civil penalties for violations of all sections of Part II of the FPA and the NGA, and augmented the Commission's existing anti-manipulation authority by expressly prohibiting manipulative acts in connection with jurisdictional transactions by "any entity," not merely sellers with market-based rate authority and blanket certificates.[17] Specifically, EPAct 2005 created new FPA section 222 and NGA section 4A, which broadly prohibited the use or employment of "any manipulative or deceptive device or contrivance" in connection with jurisdictional transactions in the electric and natural gas markets.[18] It also created new FPA section 316A and NGA section 22, which provided for maximum civil penalties of $1 million per day, per violation, for any violation of Part II of the FPA as well as any section of the NGA or any rule or order thereunder.

Crisis, it did so by enforcing certain provisions of the California Independent System Operator (CAISO) and California Power Exchange (PX) tariffs. *See Gaming Order*, 103 FERC ¶ 61,345; *San Diego Gas & Elec. Co. v. Sellers of Energy & Ancillary Servs.*, 149 FERC ¶ 61,116. Those provisions were not uniformly applicable to all jurisdictional transactions, however. Moreover, including the prohibition of manipulation directly in sellers' tariffs eliminated any questions about the relative roles of the Commission and any ISO or RTO in enforcing the terms of the applicable tariff. *See generally Am. Elec. Power Serv. Corp.*, 106 FERC ¶ 61,020 (rejecting, *inter alia*, contentions that the prohibition of manipulative gaming was impermissibly vague and that the Commission lacked authority to enforce tariff provisions that the ISO had not itself enforced).

[16] *See supra* note 3.

[17] 16 U.S.C. §§ 824v, 825o-1 (2012); 15 U.S.C. §§ 717c-1, 717t-1 (2012).

[18] EPAct 2005, Pub. L. No. 109-58, §§ 315, 1283, 119 Stat. 594, 691, 979–80 (2005) (codified as amended at 15 U.S.C. § 717c-1 and 16 U.S.C. § 824v (2012)). Congress modeled this language after the anti-fraud provision in the Securities Exchange Act of 1934, which prohibits "any manipulative or deceptive device or contrivance" in the securities markets. Order No. 670, FERC Stats. & Regs. ¶ 31,202 at P 6; *see* 15 U.S.C. § 78j(b) (2012). In some instances, the Commission has applied securities cases as precedent, but there are also instances in which the Commission has held that application of securities law is not appropriate in the context of the Commission's mandate to ensure just and reasonable rates in energy markets. *See infra* note 22.

Through notice-and-comment rulemaking, the Commission promptly implemented its expanded authority.[19] In Order No. 670, the Commission defined market manipulation broadly:

> (a) It shall be unlawful for any entity, directly or indirectly, in connection with the purchase or sale of natural gas [or electric energy] or the purchase or sale of transportation [or transmission] services subject to the jurisdiction of the Commission,
> (1) To use or employ any device, scheme, or artifice to defraud,
> (2) To make any untrue statement of a material fact or to omit to state a material fact necessary in order to make the statements made, in the light of the circumstances under which they were made, not misleading, or
> (3) To engage in any act, practice, or course of business that operates or would operate as a fraud or deceit upon any entity.[20]

The Commission outlined the elements of the Anti-Manipulation Rule in Order No. 670, explaining that it prohibits an entity from: (1) using a fraudulent device, scheme, or artifice, making a material misrepresentation or omission, or engaging in any act, practice, or course of business that operates or would operate as a fraud or deceit upon any entity; (2) with the requisite scienter; (3) in connection with the purchase or sale of natural gas or electric energy (or the transportation or transmission of such) subject to the jurisdiction of the Commission.[21]

After adoption of the Anti-Manipulation Rule, the Commission started interpreting the new law, applying it to different factual situations, and rendering decisions on the meaning of its various elements. In addition, a few federal courts have issued opinions on the new law. As a result, a law of energy market manipulation has begun to emerge. As will be discussed throughout this White Paper, this developing law is generally

---

[19] *See generally* Order No. 670, FERC Stats. & Regs. ¶ 31,202.

[20] 18 C.F.R. Part 1c (2016).

[21] Order No. 670, FERC Stats. & Regs. ¶ 31,202 at P 49. The Commission also made clear that there would be "no gap" in its prohibition of manipulation between Market Behavior Rule 2 and the Anti-Manipulation Rule, noting that the manipulative practices prohibited by Market Behavior Rule 2 "are manipulative or deceptive practices or contrivances, and are therefore prohibited activities under this Final Rule, subject to punitive and remedial action." *Id.* PP 58-59. The Commission subsequently revoked Market Behavior Rule 2 "to simplify the Commission's rules and provide greater clarity and regulatory certainty to the industry" by avoiding duplicative and overlapping requirements, but in so doing noted that its prohibitions lived on in the Anti-Manipulation Rule. *Investigation of Terms & Conditions of Public Utility Market-Based Rate Authorizations*, 114 FERC ¶ 61,165, at PP 11-12 (2006).

consistent with decades of anti-manipulation precedent in the securities and commodities context, with some differences to reflect unique characteristics of the energy markets and the Commission's obligation to ensure just and reasonable rates in such markets.[22]

This section highlights some of the key elements of this developing law on energy market manipulation:

- **Broad Definition of Fraud**: Fraud is a question of fact and is defined generally "to include any action, transaction, or conspiracy for the purpose of impairing, obstructing or defeating a well-functioning market."[23]

- **Fraud Includes Open-Market Transactions Executed With Manipulative Intent**: The Commission has held, and a United States district court has confirmed, that fraud under the Anti-Manipulation Rule includes open-market transactions, i.e., transactions occurring on public trading platforms or exchanges, executed with manipulative intent.[24]

- **Fraud Is Not Limited to Tariff and Other Explicit Rule Violations**: Fraud is determined by all the circumstances of a case, "not by a mechanical rule limiting manipulation to tariff violations."[25]

---

[22] *See, e.g.*, Order No. 670, FERC Stats. & Regs. ¶ 31,202 at P 42 (explaining that it would apply securities law on a case-by-case basis as "appropriate under the specific facts, circumstances and situations in the energy industry"); *Barclays Bank PLC*, 144 FERC ¶ 61,041, at P 58 (2013) (*Barclays*) (application of securities law cases is not always appropriate because "[t]he energy industry is not in all ways equivalent to the securities industry," and the Commission's "statutory mandate, unlike that of the SEC, is to ensure that rates for jurisdictional transactions are just and reasonable").

[23] Order No. 670, FERC Stats. & Regs. ¶ 31,202 at P 50. The Commission has explained that "the term 'well-functioning market' is not limited just to consideration of price or economically efficient outcomes in a market," but also broadly includes "the rates, terms, and conditions of service in a market." *City Power Mktg., LLC*, 152 FERC ¶ 61,012, at P 59 (2015) (*City Power*) (internal citations omitted).

[24] *Houlian Chen*, 151 FERC ¶ 61,179, at P 136 (2015) (*Chen*) (rejecting argument that transactions cannot be fraudulent if executed in "an open, transparent manner"); *FERC v. Barclays Bank PLC*, 105 F. Supp. 3d 1121, 1147 (E.D. Cal. 2015) (rejecting the argument that "trades which involve willing counterparties made on the open market cannot be actionable" (citing securities law cases)). Also, reliance is not a required element of the Anti-Manipulation Rule. *See Barclays*, 144 FERC ¶ 61,041 at P 37 n.130; *Competitive Energy Servs., LLC*, 144 FERC ¶ 61,163, at P 74 (2013) (*CES*).

[25] *In re Make-Whole Payments & Related Bidding Strategies*, 144 FERC ¶ 61,068, at P 83 (2013) (*JP Morgan*). Manipulation and tariff violations are conceptually distinct. Congress provided the Commission separate anti-manipulation authority in EPAct 2005

- **Artificial Price is Not Required**: A finding of fraud under the Anti-Manipulation Rule does not require proof that the conduct resulted in an artificial price.[26]

- **Harm is Not Required**: The Anti-Manipulation Rule contemplates cases based on attempted fraud.[27]

- **Proof of Scienter from Circumstantial Evidence**: Proof of scienter under the Anti-Manipulation Rule does not require speaking documents or other types of direct evidence.[28] Instead, it can be "established by legitimate inferences from circumstantial evidence. These inferences are based on the common knowledge of the motives and intentions of men in like circumstances."[29] Also, a manipulative purpose satisfies the scienter element even if combined with a legitimate purpose.[30]

- **Jurisdiction over Conduct Affecting FERC-Jurisdictional Transactions**: Under its "in connection with" jurisdiction, the Commission can exercise

---

and the Commission fashioned its Anti-Manipulation Rule precisely because of the need to prohibit conduct that goes beyond the terms of a tariff. *See id.*

[26] *Barclays*, 144 FERC ¶ 61,041 at P 59 ("Neither artificial price nor market power, however, is a necessary element required to find a violation of the FPA or the Anti-Manipulation Rule.").

[27] *Maxim Power Corp.*, 151 FERC ¶ 61,094, at n.5 (2015) (*Maxim Power*) (holding that "manipulation, fraud, and misrepresentations to market monitors are unacceptable in Commission-regulated markets even where such behavior is caught before it causes harm to consumers"); *see id.* (noting that Maxim Power's conduct was caught before it could cause harm and holding that "[c]ourts have long recognized that attempted manipulation and fraud are worthy of punishment in the same manner as successful schemes"); *FERC v. City Power Mktg., LLC*, No. 15-1428, 2016 WL 4250233, at *13 (D.D.C. Aug. 10, 2016) (holding that the Anti-Manipulation Rule "covers even unsuccessful schemes that harm no one"); 18 C.F.R. §§ 1c.1(a)(3), 1c.2(a)(3) (2016) (making it unlawful "[t]o engage in any act, practice, or course of business that operates *or would operate* as a fraud or deceit upon any entity" (emphasis added)).

[28] *Barclays*, 144 FERC ¶ 61,041 at P 7; *ETRACOM & Michael Rosenberg*, 155 FERC ¶ 61,284, at P 129 (2016) (*ETRACOM*).

[29] *Barclays*, 144 FERC ¶ 61,041 at P 75 (citations and quotations omitted); *accord Maxim Power*, 151 FERC ¶ 61,094 at P 88 (holding that scienter "is often proven through circumstantial evidence").

[30] *Barclays*, 144 FERC ¶ 61,041 at P 70.

jurisdiction over conduct that affects a jurisdictional transaction.[31] While the D.C. Circuit Court of Appeals has held that the Commodity Futures Trading Commission (CFTC) maintains exclusive jurisdiction over manipulative conduct occurring solely on futures exchanges,[32] the Commission has jurisdiction over manipulative transactions in FERC-jurisdictional markets or directly affecting FERC-jurisdictional prices even if those transactions benefited positions traded in a CFTC-jurisdictional market.[33]

- **Individuals are "Entities" Subject to the Anti-Manipulation Rule**: The Commission and multiple United States district courts have decided that individuals count as "entities" subject to the Anti-Manipulation Rule.[34]

III. Indicia of Fraud Under the Anti-Manipulation Rule

When adopting the Anti-Manipulation Rule, the Commission explained that "[f]raud is a question of fact that is to be determined by all the circumstances of a case."[35] In numerous orders since then, the Commission has provided guidance to industry by identifying and describing some of the key indicia it has determined to be relevant to this determination.[36] These orders are consistent with long-standing precedent in similar

---

[31] Order No. 670, FERC Stats. & Regs. ¶ 31,202 at P 22 (explaining that "in committing fraud, the entity must have intended to affect, or have acted recklessly to affect, a jurisdictional transaction").

[32] *Hunter v. FERC*, 711 F.3d 155, 157 (D.C. Cir. 2013).

[33] *See, e.g., Barclays Bank PLC*, 105 F. Supp. 3d at 1142 ("Defendants have not shown why swaps, as the benefiting position, are relevant to jurisdiction, as opposed to the trades involving physical products, from which the swaps were priced."); *FERC v. Elec. Power Supply Ass'n*, 136 S. Ct. 760, 774 (2016) (conduct that "directly affects" wholesale electric prices is within FERC jurisdiction).

[34] *See, e.g.*, Order No. 670, FERC Stats. & Regs. ¶ 31,202 at P 18; *Richard Silkman*, 144 FERC ¶ 61,164, at P 93 (2013) (Silkman); *Chen*, 151 FERC ¶ 61,179 at P 187; *Kourouma v. FERC*, 723 F.3d 274 (D.C. Cir. 2012) (upholding Commission's assessment of civil penalty); *FERC v. Silkman*, Nos. 13-13054-DPW, 13-13056-DPW, 2016 WL 1430009, at *20 (D. Mass. Apr. 11, 2016); *Barclays Bank PLC*, 105 F. Supp. 3d at 1146; *City Power Mktg.*, No. 15-1428, 2016 WL 4250233, at *15; *FERC v. Maxim Power Corp.*, No. 15-30113, 2016 WL 4126378, at *14 (D. Mass. July 21, 2016).

[35] Order No. 670, FERC Stats. & Regs. ¶ 31,202 at P 50.

[36] *See, e.g., Barclays*, 144 FERC ¶ 61,041 at P 32; *Constellation Energy Commodities Grp., Inc.*, 138 FERC ¶ 61,168, at PP 7–10 (2012) (*Constellation*); *CES*, 144 FERC ¶ 61,163 at PP 43–54; *Deutsche Bank Energy Trading, LLC*, 142 FERC ¶ 61,056, at PP 19–20 (2013) (*Deutsche Bank*); *Chen*, 151 FERC ¶ 61,179 at PP 69–93;

contexts, as courts have considered many of the same indicia for years in interpreting anti-fraud statutes in securities and commodities law. By describing these indicia, the Commission has provided valuable guidance to market participants on the types of actions and behaviors that can lead to a finding of energy market manipulation. Such guidance allows market participants to better monitor, detect, cease, and report potentially manipulative conduct. Although it is not possible to provide an exhaustive list of indicia of fraudulent conduct for the reasons described below (in section IV), this section highlights the Commission's discussion of three of these indicia.

A. Illicit Purpose of Conduct

The Commission considers the purpose of an entity's actions as a critical factor in determining whether conduct is fraudulent under the Anti-Manipulation Rule. The Commission has focused on this factor since issuing Order No. 670, explaining that fraud includes "any action, transaction, or conspiracy for the *purpose* of impairing, obstructing, or defeating a well-functioning market."[37] In subsequent orders, the Commission built on this language, making clear that the purpose underlying market behavior can determine whether that behavior is fraudulent or lawful.[38]

For example, in *Brian Hunter*, the Commission found that sales of natural gas futures contracts on NYMEX were fraudulent because they were executed "for the

---

City Power, 152 FERC ¶ 61,012 at PP 92–114; *Coaltrain Energy, L.P.*, 155 FERC ¶ 61,204, at PP 122-144, 149-168, 174-193 (2016) (*Coaltrain*); *ETRACOM*, 155 FERC ¶ 61,284 at PP 97-131. These indicia are not legal elements or claims, but, rather, general factors the Commission has considered in determining whether conduct meets the fraud element.

[37] Order No. 670, FERC Stats. & Regs. ¶ 31,202 at P 50 (emphasis added).

[38] *See, e.g.*, *Coaltrain*, 155 FERC ¶ 61,204 at P 5 ("Respondents' OCL Trades were manipulative because they were executed for the sole or primary purpose of targeting and garnering MLSA payments."); *City Power*, 152 FERC ¶ 61,012 at P 103; *Chen*, 151 FERC ¶ 61,179 at P 80. This focus on purpose parallels years of precedent under anti-fraud provisions in the securities and commodities contexts. *See, e.g.*, *Koch v. SEC*, 793 F.3d 147, 153–154 (D.C. Cir. 2015) ("And intent—not success—is all that must accompany manipulative conduct to prove a violation of the Exchange Act and its implementing regulations."); *Markowski v. SEC*, 274 F.3d 525, 529 (D.C. Cir. 2001) (holding that conduct can be manipulative "solely because of the actor's purpose"); *City Power Mktg.*, No. 15-1428, 2016 WL 4250233, at *12 (citing *Koch* and *Markowski* in recognizing that "securities traders are not free to trade for whatever purpose they wish"); *In re Amaranth Natural Gas Commodities Litig.*, 587 F. Supp. 2d 513, 534 (S.D.N.Y. 2008) (holding that "a legitimate transaction combined with an improper motive is commodities manipulation").

purposes of controlling prices."[39] In reaching this conclusion, the Commission explained that the "difference between legitimate open-market transactions and illegal open-market transactions may be nothing more than a trader's manipulative purpose for executing such transactions."[40] Similarly, in *Barclays*, the Commission found the bank's uneconomic power trades to be fraudulent because the company entered into the trades for the "purpose of moving the Index price at a particular point so that Barclays' financial swap positions at that same trading point would benefit."[41]

Most recently, in three orders addressing Up-To Congestion (UTC) trades in PJM Interconnection, LLC (PJM), the Commission made its most pronounced statement on the importance of purpose in its fraud determinations. The Commission explained the purpose of UTC trading in PJM—to arbitrage day-ahead and real-time congestion prices—and then examined the purpose behind the respondents' UTC trades, finding that their trades "were neither consistent with how the UTC product historically traded nor aligned with the arbitrage purpose of those trades."[42] The Commission elaborated,

> Speculative UTC trades placed to arbitrage price spreads will have as their sole or primary price signal the price risk of the underlying UTC spread and will be placed with the purpose of profiting based on the direction of the spread. Yet, despite the market purpose behind UTCs and despite [Respondents'] articulated understanding of that purpose, Respondents engaged in round-trip UTC trades that had no relationship to this purpose.[43]

---

[39] *Brian Hunter*, 135 FERC ¶ 61,054, at P 49 (2011), *order denying reh'g*, 137 FERC ¶ 61,146 (2011), *rev'd on other grounds sub nom, Hunter v. FERC*, 711 F.3d 155 (D.C. Cir. 2013).

[40] *Id.* P 50.

[41] *Barclays*, 144 FERC ¶ 61,041 at P 2.

[42] *Coaltrain*, 155 FERC ¶ 61,204 at PP 166, 191; *City Power*, 152 FERC ¶ 61,012 at P 103; *Chen*, 151 FERC ¶ 61,179 at P 80. *See also In re PJM Up-To Congestion Transactions.*, 142 FERC ¶ 61,088 (2013) (approving settlement with Oceanside Power, LLC and trader Robert Scavo related to UTC trading).

[43] *Chen*, 151 FERC ¶ 61,179 at P 80. "'Round-trip' UTC trades canceled each other out by placing the first leg of the trade from locations A to B, and simultaneously placing a second leg of equal volume from locations B to A." *Id.* P 3. *See also Coaltrain*, 155 FERC ¶ 61,204 at P 103; *City Power*, 152 FERC ¶ 61,012 at P 103. The U.S. District Court for the District of Columbia in *City Power Marketing* also highlighted the importance of purpose, noting that "the same conduct may or may not be deceptive

Given the Commission's guidance that purpose is a critical factor in determining fraudulent behavior, entities should consider requiring employees to document and articulate the purpose behind any conduct that is likely to raise red flags so that compliance departments can vet the conduct and ensure that employees have a legitimate reason for it.[44] For example, in *Constellation*, a case that involved trading virtual products for the purpose of influencing day-ahead prices, the company agreed in a Commission-approved settlement to institute a new procedure "to document the purpose of virtual transactions."[45]

B. Uneconomic Conduct

The Commission considers the uneconomic nature of conduct as another important factor in its determinations of what constitutes fraud. Uneconomic conduct occurs when an entity knowingly engages in behavior that loses money on a stand-alone basis—or is indifferent to whether it loses money—but engages in the behavior anyway to serve an ulterior purpose (e.g., to move prices in a way that benefits related financial positions). As with other indicia, the Commission explains that "standing alone [profitability] is neither necessary nor dispositive," but "is an indicium to be considered among the overall facts that the Commission examines when considering a potential violation of its Anti-Manipulation Rule."[46] The Commission has considered the uneconomic nature of conduct as one of the bases for finding fraud in several orders assessing penalties for different types of manipulative conduct.[47] The Commission has also approved multiple

---

depending on an actor's purpose." *City Power Mktg.*, No. 15-1428, 2016 WL 4250233, at *12.

[44] *See* Compliance Practices White Paper at section IV.B.1.

[45] *Constellation*, 138 FERC ¶ 61,168 at P 23.

[46] *Barclays*, 144 FERC ¶ 61,041 at P 43. *See also Deutsche Bank*, 142 FERC ¶ 61,056 at P 20 ("Deutsche Bank's physical transactions were not profitable. Even if these physical transactions had been profitable, however, profitability is not determinative on the question of manipulation and does not inoculate trading from any potential manipulation claim (although profitability may be relevant in assessing the conduct).").

[47] *See, e.g., BP America, Inc.*, 156 FERC ¶ 61,031, at PP 22, 131-34 (2016) (*BP*) (holding that uneconomic trading is one indicia of manipulative activity and finding relevant to the manipulative scheme that Respondents lost money on certain physical trading and transportation until they became aware that compliance would be monitoring such trading, after which their trading became overall profitable); *Coaltrain*, 155 FERC ¶ 61,204 at PP 135, 163, 188 (holding that Respondents' trades were routinely unprofitable and quantifying the losses of the trades); *City Power*, 152 FERC ¶ 61,012 at P 101 (holding in a matter involving gaming of market rules that respondents' trading "was uneconomic, which supports the conclusion that a course of business and a scheme to defraud existed"); *CES*, 144 FERC ¶ 61,163 at P 43 and *Silkman*, 144 FERC ¶ 61,164 at

settlements for violations of the Anti-Manipulation Rule where entities engaged in uneconomic behavior.[48] These orders' consideration of the uneconomic nature of conduct comports with anti-fraud precedent in other contexts.[49]

Because uneconomic trading is one sign of fraudulent conduct, compliance departments at trading companies should consider monitoring and reviewing their traders' profit and loss calculations, particularly for instances in which a trader is accepting persistent losses in a price-setting product while simultaneously having exposure to a position whose value is tied to such trading.[50] Managers and compliance professionals should be concerned, or at least ask questions, about any behavior where the company appears indifferent to profit and loss considerations.

P 43 (holding in parallel cases involving misrepresentations that a respondent's decision to curtail power from a generator over a five-day period "was uneconomic given [its] ability and established practice of generating electricity [from that generator] at lower cost"); *Lincoln Paper & Tissue, LLC*, 144 FERC ¶ 61,162, at P 30 (2013) (*Lincoln*) (same holding in similar case); *Barclays*, 144 FERC ¶ 61,041 at P 43 (holding in cross-market manipulation case that "Respondents' trading was generally uneconomic and this factor is considered among all of the circumstances of the case in reaching the conclusion that a fraudulent scheme existed").

[48] *See, e.g., Constellation*, 138 FERC ¶ 61,168 at P 8 (noting that traders' virtual and physical transactions "were routinely unprofitable"); *JP Morgan*, 144 FERC ¶ 61,068 at P 43 (explaining that JP Morgan "lost millions of dollars at market rates," but profited overall based on external payments); *MISO Virtual & FTR Trading*, 146 FERC ¶ 61,072, at P 4 (2014) (noting that traders experienced "losses on heavy virtual trading").

[49] *See, e.g., Markowski*, 274 F.3d at 529 (affirming Securities and Exchange Commission's market manipulation determination based, in part, on finding that the company's "prospects of losing some money . . . in the short run . . . was worth the benefit of keeping its customers and preserving confidence in its other stocks"); *Crane Co. v. Westinghouse Air Brake Co.*, 419 F.2d 787, 795 (2d Cir. 1969) (holding that company's "massive buying . . . coupled with its concealed sales, was not consistent with the normal desire of an investor to buy at as low a price as possible" (internal citations and quotations omitted)).

[50] *See, e.g.*, Compliance Practices White Paper at section IV.B.2 ("[I]f a trader is engaging in a scheme that involves losing money in a price-setting product, such as virtual transactions in an organized electric market, to benefit a financial position that is settled off of the price being targeted, an effective way to identify this behavior might be to monitor the trader's virtual PnL, at each location, for persistent losses or a pattern of losses.").

C. Conduct Inconsistent with Market Fundamentals

The Commission's fraud determinations also consider whether conduct is consistent with market fundamentals of supply and demand. As is true in other markets, prices in energy markets are driven by certain underlying factors affecting the supply and demand for a product. The Commission has made clear that participants in energy markets should have as their price signal these supply and demand fundamentals, not ancillary considerations that bear no relation to underlying market fundamentals. For example, participants in the physical markets should be aiming to maximize their returns on the primary energy product based on supply and demand factors, not on secondary considerations, such as make-whole payments. Similarly, participants speculating in the financial markets should express a market view based on their knowledge of market forces and conditions—including weather, outages, and supply and load forecasts—not based on a desire to capture some unrelated revenue stream.[51] Likewise, arbitrage should be aimed at anticipated prices of underlying products based on trading acumen and market fundamentals, not at market rules that can be exploited to profit with little to no risk.[52] In short, competitive energy markets exist to provide products at competitive rates based on fundamental factors of supply and demand, and participants should be trading consistent with this purpose.

In *Barclays*, for example, the Commission found that the traders entered into daily power transactions "not based on normal supply and demand fundamentals, but rather on the intent to . . . benefit [their] Financial Swaps."[53] The Commission explained that this type of trading, devoid of supply and demand considerations, is fraudulent because it "inject[s] inaccurate information into the market and impair[s] the functioning of the Commission-regulated physical markets."[54] Similarly, in approving a settlement in *Deutsche Bank*, the Commission noted that the company's "physical trades were not consistent with the fundamentals underlying the market price . . . e.g., supply and

---

[51] Staff recognizes that market participants engage in hedging transactions to offset the risk of another position such as an asset already owned by the market participant. Transactions that are undertaken without manipulative intent and with a legitimate hedging purpose are not manipulative.

[52] *See, e.g.*, *Chen*, 151 FERC ¶ 61,179 at P 80 ("Speculative UTC trades placed to arbitrage price spreads will have as their sole or primary price signal the price risk of the underlying UTC spread and will be placed with the purpose of profiting based on the direction of the spread."); *City Power*, 152 FERC ¶ 61,012 at P 103 (same); *Coaltrain*, 155 FERC ¶ 61,204 at P 103 (same).

[53] *Barclays*, 144 FERC ¶ 61,041 at P 57; *accord City Power*, 152 FERC ¶ 61,012 at P 129 (finding that traders placed UTC trades "without regard to market fundamentals of supply and demand").

[54] *Barclays*, 144 FERC ¶ 61,041 at P 57.

15

demand, but rather were undertaken with the intent to change the value of [its related positions]. Deutsche Bank thus injected false and deceptive information into the marketplace . . . ."[55]

The Commission's view on the relevance of market fundamentals in energy trading is consistent with securities cases that have held that deception occurs when participants artificially affect the market by injecting false supply and demand information.[56]

IV.   Types of Market Manipulation

It is not possible to provide an exhaustive list of all types of manipulation because determining whether certain conduct constitutes manipulation is a fact-specific inquiry. Moreover, market participants are increasingly sophisticated, and "[t]he methods and techniques of manipulation are limited only by the ingenuity of man."[57] Manipulative schemes are ever-changing and, as a result, the Commission cannot detect all forms of manipulation in advance. Similarly, the tariffs that establish and govern complex energy markets do not and cannot cover all forms of conduct to be prohibited in advance.[58]

Thus, a static list of prohibited types of conduct would not work for energy markets. This is why Congress granted the Commission a flexible, broad, and dynamic

---

[55] *Deutsche Bank*, 142 FERC ¶ 61,056 at P 19.

[56] *See, e.g., Gurary v. Winehouse*, 190 F.3d 37, 45 (2d Cir. 1999) ("The gravamen of manipulation is deception of investors into believing that prices at which they purchase and sell securities are determined by the natural interplay of supply and demand, not rigged by manipulators."); *Crane*, 419 F.2d at 794 ("[H]onest markets are made by the balancing of investment demand and investment supply."); *SEC v. Kwak*, No. 3:04-cv-1331, 2008 WL 410427, at *4 (D. Conn. Feb. 12, 2008) (holding conduct "plainly . . . deceptive under section 10(b) because it tricks investors into believing that the reported prices for [the] stock reflect transactions that are solely the product of independent forces of supply and demand"); *see also City Power Mktg.*, No. 15-1428, 2016 WL 4250233, at *12 (noting that securities traders "are presumed to be trading on the basis of their best estimates of a security's underlying economic value").

[57] *Cargill, Inc. v. Hardin*, 452 F.2d 1154, 1163 (8th Cir. 1971); *see also JP Morgan*, 144 FERC ¶ 61,068 at P 83 (noting "the impossibility of foreseeing the 'myriad means' of misconduct in which market participants may engage" (citing *Cargill*)); *Chen*, 151 FERC ¶ 61,179 at P 120 (citing *Cargill*).

[58] *See JP Morgan*, 144 FERC ¶ 61,068 at P 83 ("fraud is a question of fact to be determined by all the circumstances of the case, not by a mechanical rule limiting manipulation to tariff violations" (citation omitted)).

statutory framework to prohibit and penalize such conduct. As the Commission explained in the aftermath of the Western Energy Crisis:

> Enron (and others) would demand that a regulatory agency have the prescience to include in a rate schedule all specific misconduct in which a particular market participant could conceivably engage. That standard is unrealistic and would render regulatory agencies impotent to address newly conceived misconduct and allow them only to pursue, to phrase it simply, last year's misconduct – essentially, to continually fight the last war and deny the capability to fight the present or next one.[59]

Nonetheless, this White Paper provides guidance on some of the types of conduct the Commission has determined, up to this point, constitute manipulation. Combined with sound judgment and an institutional commitment to compliance, this guidance, along with the Commission orders on which it is based, the Compliance Practices White Paper, and other sources such as the Office of Enforcement Annual Reports, should allow market participants and compliance departments to be able to detect manipulative conduct or, in closer cases, ask tough questions about conduct that appears problematic.[60]

---

[59] *Am. Elec. Power Serv. Corp.*, 106 FERC ¶ 61,020 at P 45 (emphasis in original). Similarly, market participants do not get a "first bite" or "free pass" just because they discover and engage in a novel, unique form of manipulation. *BP*, 156 FERC ¶ 61,031 at P 46 n.87 ("[N]ovel schemes or methods do not provide immunity from the Anti-Manipulation Rule in the Commission-regulated markets" (citations omitted)); *see also United States v. Arcadipane*, 41 F.3d 1, 5 (1st Cir. 1994) ("Fair warning . . . does not mean that the first bite is free, nor does the doctrine demand an explicit or personalized warning."); *Superintendent of Ins. v. Bankers Life & Cas. Co.*, 404 U.S. 6, 10 n.7 (1971) ("[We do not] think it sound to dismiss a complaint merely because the alleged scheme does not involve the type of fraud that is 'usually associated with the sale or purchase of securities.' We believe that § 10b and Rule 10b-5 prohibit all fraudulent schemes in connection with the purchase or sale of securities, whether the artifices employed involve a garden type variety of fraud, or present a unique form of deception. Novel or atypical methods should not provide immunity from the securities laws." (citation omitted)).

[60] Entities can also consult with Enforcement staff before engaging in conduct that they understand poses a risk of manipulation. *See, e.g.*, *Chen*, 151 FERC ¶ 61,179 at P 186 n.408 (explaining that the respondent did not seek guidance from staff about their round-trip trading and holding that he "reasonably knew or should have known that his round-trip trading scheme raised potential compliance concerns and, at a minimum, should have inquired further into the lawfulness of his behavior"). Although Enforcement staff cannot provide formal decisions that bind the Commission, it can in

A. Cross-Market Manipulation Schemes

Cross-market manipulation involves trading in one market with the intent to move prices in a particular direction to benefit positions in a related market. This type of scheme occurred during the Western Energy Crisis and continues today in securities and commodities markets, as well as both the electric and natural gas markets. For example, recent electric cross-market cases have involved trading physical or virtual power to influence Financial Transmission Rights (FTR), also known as financial Congestion Revenue Rights (CRR), financial swap positions, or a market participant's overall generation fleet. Cross-market manipulation cases in the gas context have involved trading physical gas to affect published index prices that benefit related financial positions tied to those same index prices.

1. Pre-EPAct 2005 Cross-Market Manipulation Schemes

During the Western Energy Crisis, market participants misreported price and volume trade data for certain price-setting products in physical natural gas markets (e.g., physical fixed-price or physical basis gas) to move published index prices in order to benefit a financial position. For example, five trading companies admitted to reporting false information to index publishers during the Western Energy Crisis regarding their trading volumes and prices for certain price-setting physical natural gas products.[61] These companies took these actions in the physical markets for the purpose of moving prices to "enhance the value of financial positions" in a related market.[62]

---

most instances at least informally discuss its views, including factors it might consider in determining whether it believes the relevant conduct constitutes manipulation. Moreover, the Commission provides a No Action Letter process, which provides entities an opportunity to obtain written advice as to whether staff would recommend that the Commission take no enforcement action with respect to specific conduct. *See Interpretative Order Regarding No-Action Letter Process*, 113 FERC ¶ 61,174 (2005); *Interpretative Order Modifying No-Action Letter Process*, 117 FERC ¶ 61,069 (2006); *Obtaining Guidance on Regulatory Requirements*, 123 FERC ¶ 61,157 (2008). In addition, entities may file a petition for a declaratory order to obtain more formal, binding guidance from the Commission.

[61] *Final Report on Price Manipulation in Western Markets*, at ES-6.

[62] *Id. See also In re Dynegy Mktg. & Trade & West Coast Power LLC*, CFTC Docket No. 03-03, at *3 (Dec. 18, 2002) ($5 million settlement with CFTC for misreporting price and volume data in the physical market to benefit related financial positions); *In re El Paso Merch. Energy, L.P.*, CFTC Docket No. 03-09, at *2 (Mar. 26, 2003) ($20 million settlement with CFTC for misreporting trade information and withholding information about actual trades).

2. Post-EPAct 2005 Cross-Market Manipulation Schemes

Following EPAct 2005, both electric and gas cross-market manipulation cases have involved interrelated markets in which market participants trade in one market with the intent to move prices in a particular direction to benefit positions in a related market. In these cases, companies have exhibited some or many of the following warning signs, which have been relevant to the Commission's finding of manipulation: large market shares in price-setting instruments; trading in the physical markets in a direction that benefits a simultaneously held position in a related market; benefiting positions that have exposure to related physical trading; trading large volumes in the physical market without accumulating much of a net position; and physical trading with consistent losses or an indifference to price. The Commission has used its anti-manipulation authority and enhanced penalty authority to sanction this harmful conduct. In the process, the Commission has provided valuable guidance on the warning signs indicative of a cross-market scheme.

a. Electric Cases

Recent cross-market manipulation schemes in electric markets generally fall into two categories: (1) *physical* trading for the purpose of benefiting financial swap positions or congestion-related financial positions (such as FTRs); and (2) *virtual* trading for the purpose of benefiting financial swap positions or congestion-related financial positions. Outside either of these categories, one case involved trading a physical product to benefit the entity's generation fleet.

In *Barclays*, illustrating the first "physical-for-financial" cross-market manipulation category, the Commission found that Barclays engaged in manipulative physical trading to benefit its financial swap positions.[63] Specifically, the Commission found that Barclays' traders built substantial monthly physical index positions in the opposite direction of their financial swap positions they assembled at the same points. Then, to "flatten" their physical index obligations at those points, they traded a next-day fixed-price or "cash" product to increase or lower the daily index (to which their next-day fixed-price trades contributed). Thus, Barclays made its physical fixed-price trades not to profit from the relationship between market fundamentals of supply and demand, but as part of a scheme to move the daily index price by injecting false supply and demand information to benefit its financial swap positions.[64] The 2014 *MISO Cinergy Hub Transactions* investigation involved a similar strategy of scheduling and trading physical power into and out of Midcontinent Independent System Operator (MISO)-operated

---

[63] *Barclays,* 144 FERC ¶ 61,041.

[64] *Id.* P 2.

19

markets to benefit related financial swap positions that settled off of real-time MISO prices.[65]

Deutsche Bank also involved a physical-for-financial electric cross-market manipulation scheme.[66] In that case, the Commission approved a settlement based on staff's finding that Deutsche Bank traded its physical exports at the Silver Peak intertie with the intent to benefit its financial CRR positions at Silver Peak. In doing so, staff found that Deutsche Bank injected false and deceptive information into the marketplace and affected the price at Silver Peak, thus hindering the proper functioning of the physical market at Silver Peak as well as the CRR market.[67] As described by the Commission, prior to engaging in the physical transactions at issue in the case, the CRR traders had focused exclusively on bidding on CRRs and had no responsibility for physical trading.[68] Further, Deutsche Bank lost money on its physical transactions on every day that it traded at Silver Peak during the relevant period.[69]

Constellation highlights the second category of electric cross-market manipulation—using virtual trades to benefit financial positions. In that case, Constellation entered into virtual and physical transactions to impact day-ahead prices in the New York Independent System Operator (NYISO) and ISO-New England (ISO-NE) markets to benefit its financial positions that included financial swaps, FTRs, and transmission congestion contracts.[70] As described in the Commission order approving the settlement agreement, Constellation's virtual and physical transactions at issue were "routinely unprofitable."[71] In addition, staff found relevant to its determination of manipulation that such transactions exhibited a "repetitive pattern" of being scheduled in a direction that benefited Constellation's financial positions, and that the size of Constellation's swap positions was significant, thus incentivizing the manipulative

---

[65] *MISO Cinergy Hub Transactions*, 149 FERC ¶ 61,278 (2014). As stipulated in the settlement agreement (attached to the Order approving it), the traders consistently flowed physical power in the direction of their financial swaps with the intent to move prices. Also, the traders' physical flows were occasionally profitable but lost significant money over time, and on days of manipulative trading, gains from the swaps exceeded the losses from the physical flows—further incentivizing the manipulative scheme. *Id.,* Settlement Agreement at PP 20–23.

[66] *Deutsche Bank*, 142 FERC ¶ 61,056.

[67] *Id.* P 19.

[68] *Id.* P 3.

[69] *Id.* P 15.

[70] *Constellation*, 138 FERC ¶ 61,168.

[71] *Id.* P 8.

conduct.[72] Similarly, in *MISO Virtual & FTR Trading*, Louis Dreyfus Energy Services L.P. made virtual supply offers or demand bids at a loss to benefit related FTR positions.[73] In the order approving settlement, "[t]he Commission emphasize[d] that using virtual trades to create artificial congestion in the Day-Ahead market for the purpose of enhancing the value of FTR positions violates the Commission's Anti-Manipulation Rule."[74]

The Commission's recent order assessing civil penalties in *ETRACOM* also falls into this category of cross-market schemes: ETRACOM submitted $0 or negatively-priced virtual supply offers to lower the day-ahead price and increase the profitability of its related financial CRR positions.[75] In finding manipulation, the Commission rejected ETRACOM's arguments that CAISO's flawed market design and software errors rendered their virtual trading behavior permissible, finding instead that "market design flaws do not excuse manipulative conduct and sometimes provide the context for it."[76]

While most electric cross-market cases fall into the foregoing two categories, another type of scheme, addressed in *Gila River Power LLC* and also discussed *infra* at section IV.C.2, involved manipulating physical products to benefit the company's generation fleet which sold its power as imports into the CAISO at the Palo Verde intertie. In conjunction with bidding its generation in the day-ahead market at the Palo Verde intertie, the company scheduled physical wheeling-through transactions into CAISO.[77] Gila River used the wheeling-through transactions to increase the amount of generated power it could import at Palo Verde as sales and to increase the corresponding sales price of those generation imports by alleviating congestion.[78] Once the day-ahead market settled, Gila River bought back the wheeling-through transaction, effectively cancelling it. The scheme allowed Gila River to import the maximum amount of power possible across the intertie and raised the prices at which it sold those imports.[79]

b. *Natural Gas Cases*

In the natural gas arena post EPAct 2005, cross-market manipulation schemes have involved trading physical fixed-price or basis gas to affect published index prices

---

[72] *Id.* PP 5, 7.

[73] *MISO Virtual & FTR Trading*, 146 FERC ¶ 61,072 at PP 4-5.

[74] *Id.* P 13.

[75] *ETRACOM*, 155 FERC ¶ 61,284.

[76] *Id.* PP 118-127.

[77] *Gila River Power LLC*, 141 FERC ¶ 61,136, at PP 8-10, 13 (2012) (*Gila River*).

[78] *Id.*

[79] *Id.*

that benefit related financial positions tied to those same index prices. The *Energy Transfer Partners L.P.* case provides an example of such conduct.[80] In 2009, the Commission approved a settlement based on staff's finding that ETP sold monthly fixed-price gas at the Houston Ship Channel (HSC) during bidweek to suppress the Platts *Inside* FERC (IFERC) HSC monthly index price to benefit ETP's physical and financial positions that profited from a lower HSC IFERC index.

The recent *BP America, Inc.* (*BP*) case is another example of a natural gas cross-market manipulation scheme.[81] In that case, the Commission found that BP engaged in physical next-day fixed-price trading at HSC with the intent to suppress the Platts HSC *Gas Daily* index to benefit its related financial spread positions that profited from a lower HSC *Gas Daily* index.[82] The Commission found that BP's traders changed their trading and transportation patterns (including using transportation uneconomically and engaging in early, volume-heavy selling at aggressively low prices) in a way that benefited those financial positions and incurred losses, with "no reasonable explanation for the[] changes."[83]

Direct Energy involved another fraudulent scheme to manipulate the *Gas Daily* index price.[84] Direct Energy self-reported that certain of its traders sold next-day fixed-price gas to lower the *Gas Daily* index, while simultaneously holding financial positions that benefited from this lower index price.[85] Direct Energy also reported that it lost money on those transactions, and that most of that trading occurred very early in the day when the markets were relatively illiquid.[86]

Most recently, the Commission approved two settlement agreements based on Enforcement staff's findings that National Energy & Trade, L.P. (National Energy) and one of its traders engaged in a cross-market scheme by trading physical natural gas

---

[80] *Energy Transfer Partners L.P.*, 128 FERC ¶ 61,269 (2009). Staff sought penalties against ETP under the anti-manipulation rule at the time, 18 C.F.R. § 284.403(a) (2005), which was promulgated under the NGA after the Western Energy Crisis, but was subsequently rescinded by the Commission in 2006 after Congress passed EPAct 2005. *Id.* P 14.

[81] *BP,* 156 FERC ¶ 61,031.

[82] *Id.* PP 2-3, 16.

[83] *Id.* PP 140-141.

[84] *Direct Energy Servs., LLC*, 148 FERC ¶ 61,114 (2014) (*Direct Energy*); *see infra* section V.A. (further discussion of *Direct Energy* in the context of compliance and the Penalty Guidelines).

[85] *Direct Energy*, 148 FERC ¶ 61,114 at P 9.

[86] *Id.* PP 8–9.

products to benefit related financial positions at the Tetco M3 trading location.[87] Enforcement staff found that National Energy and its trader lost money on their physical transactions, but that such losses helped to lower index prices to their benefit.[88] As part of the settlement agreement, the trader agreed to a one-year trading ban.[89]

B. Gaming of Market Rules

Gaming is another type of conduct that the Commission has determined can constitute market manipulation, and has prohibited for years. The Commission has described gaming strategies in orders stemming from the Western Energy Crisis and more recent manipulation cases. In those orders, discussed further in this section, the Commission has made clear that gaming includes behavior that circumvents or takes unfair advantage of market rules or conditions in a deceptive manner that harms the proper functioning of the market and potentially other market participants or consumers. This is reflected in the Commission's broad definition of fraud.

1. Pre-EPAct 2005 Gaming Schemes

The Commission found many of the schemes that occurred during the Western Energy Crisis to be "gaming," as that term was defined in the CAISO and California PX tariffs under their tariffs' Market Monitoring and Information Protocol (MMIP). The MMIP defined gaming as "taking unfair advantage of the rules and procedures set forth in the PX and ISO tariffs, Protocols or Activity Rules . . . to the detriment of the efficiency of, and of consumers in, the ISO Markets."[90] For example, the Commission, in its 2003 *Gaming Order*, recognized several congestion-related practices as gaming behavior such as circular scheduling, or "Death Star," which involved scheduling a counterflow to receive a congestion relief payment, and then simultaneously scheduling

---

[87] *National Energy & Trade, L.P.*, 156 FERC ¶ 61,154 (2016) (*National Energy*); *In re David Silva*, 156 FERC ¶ 61,155 (2016) (*Silva*). National Energy's settlement also covered its trading at HSC, Transco Zone 6 (New York), and Henry Hub. *National Energy*, 156 FERC ¶ 61,154 at P 1.

[88] *National Energy*, 156 FERC ¶ 61,154 at P 10; *Silva*, 156 FERC ¶ 61,155 at P 10.

[89] *Silva*, 156 FERC ¶ 61,155 at P 17.

[90] ISO MMIP 2.1.3. The MMIP also defined gaming to include "taking undue advantage of other conditions that may affect the availability of transmission and generation capacity . . . or actions and behaviors that may otherwise render the system and the ISO Markets vulnerable to price manipulation to the detriment of their efficiency." *Id.* The MMIP formed part of the CAISO and PX tariffs. *Gaming Order*, 103 FERC ¶ 61,345 at PP 16–17. The Commission found that the MMIP put parties on notice as to what practices would be subject to monitoring and potentially corrective or enforcement action. *Id.* P 23.

flow outside the CAISO control area (which the CAISO could not "see") to complete a "loop" with the counterflow such that no actual power was moved and congestion was not relieved.[91] The practice thus entailed scheduling transactions that, taken together, eliminated any risk (with no net flow) for the purpose of obtaining a congestion relief payment. The Commission found that such congestion schemes involved "false schedules," "fraudulent[] recei[pt of] congestion relief payments," and "false representations."[92]

Another type of gaming behavior, called Paper Trading (and referred to by market participants generally as "Get Shorty") involved market participants' sales of ancillary services into the day-ahead market without first procuring the necessary capacity to provide such services. If called upon by CAISO to provide such services, the entities would purchase the ancillary services at a lower price in the real-time market, profiting by buying the services at a lower real-time price than their day-ahead market bid. The Commission reasoned that this behavior constituted gaming because the market participants took unfair advantage of the market rules by using false representations and/or receiving payments for services they did not have the capacity to provide.[93]

Following the 2003 *Gaming Order*, the Commission prohibited additional gaming practices through its Market Behavior Rules that sellers were required to comply with as a condition of their market-based rate authority.[94] Market Behavior Rule 2 expressly prohibited wash trades, defined as "pre-arranged offsetting trades of the same product among the same parties, which involve no economic risk and no net change in beneficial ownership."[95] The rule also prohibited transactions predicated on submitting false information to transmission providers or other entities responsible for operating the

---

[91] *Gaming Order*, 103 FERC ¶ 61,345 at P 43; *San Diego Gas & Elec. Co.*, 149 FERC ¶ 61,116 at P 186 n.416.

[92] *Gaming Order*, 103 FERC ¶ 61,345 at P 46.

[93] *See id.* PP 48–51. The Commission also suggested ways that market participants could potentially show that the Paper Trading transactions were legitimate transactions, for example, by showing that the resources to provide the ancillary services sold in the day-ahead market were actually available to the bidder. *Id.* P 68. In 2014, the Commission identified additional conduct during the Western Energy Crisis that was not identified in its 2003 *Gaming Order* but that also violated CAISO's MMIP "gaming" provision. That conduct included certain anomalous bidding behavior and sales of ancillary services without first procuring the underlying capacity. *San Diego Gas & Elec. Co.*, 149 FERC ¶ 61,116 at PP 86, 94, 99.

[94] *Investigation of Terms and Conditions of Public Utility Market-Based Rate Authorizations*, 105 FERC ¶ 61,218.

[95] *Id.* P 52.

transmission grid. Additionally, the rule addressed some of the congestion-related gaming that occurred during the Western Energy Crisis by prohibiting transactions in which an entity first creates artificial congestion and then purports to relieve such artificial congestion.[96] Finally, the rule extended beyond gaming behavior, generally prohibiting collusion with another party for the purpose of manipulating market prices, market conditions, or market rules for electric energy or electricity products.[97]

2. Post-EPAct 2005 Gaming Schemes

The Commission has recognized that one of the primary objectives of EPAct 2005 was to deter the type of gaming schemes that occurred during the Western Energy Crisis. Specifically, the Commission has recognized that one of its core responsibilities under EPAct 2005 is "detecting, preventing, and appropriately sanctioning the gaming of the energy markets."[98] In Order No. 670, the Commission expressly stated that it was incorporating Market Behavior Rule 2, which addressed the prohibited behavior and transactions described above, including gaming behavior, into its Anti-Manipulation Rule.[99] As the Commission reasoned, "these are examples of prohibited manipulation, all of which are manipulative or deceptive devices or contrivances, and are therefore prohibited activities under this Final Rule."[100] As described below, following EPAct 2005, the Commission has carried out Congress's intent to use the new anti-manipulation authority to prohibit and sanction the type of gaming schemes that plagued energy markets during the Western Energy Crisis.

Since EPAct 2005, the Commission has ruled in several cases that provide guidance on the types of trading behavior that are considered gaming and prohibited under the Anti-Manipulation Rule. These Commission orders are consistent with the Commission's pre-EPAct 2005 findings on gaming practices, which emphasize that gaming includes effectively riskless transactions executed for the purpose of receiving a collateral benefit;[101] conduct that is inconsistent or interferes with a market design

---

[96] *Id.* PP 76–77.

[97] *Id.* P 85.

[98] *See, e.g., JP Morgan*, 144 FERC ¶ 61,068 at P 87.

[99] *See* Order No. 670, FERC Stats. & Regs. ¶ 31,202 at PP 58–59.

[100] *Id.* P 59. The following year, the Commission rescinded Market Behavior Rule 2 as unnecessary, citing Order No. 670: "As we stated in issuing the new anti-manipulation rule, the specifically prohibited actions in Rule 2 . . . all are prohibited activities under new section 1c.2 of our regulations . . . ." *Investigation of Terms & Conditions of Pub. Util. Market-Based Rate Authorizations*, 114 FERC ¶ 61,165 at P 24.

[101] The Commission has indicated that raising a mere theoretical risk is not sufficient, by itself, to defeat a market manipulation claim. *See Chen*, 151 FERC ¶ 61,179 at P 104 (rejecting respondents' argument that their UTC transactions had some

function; and conduct that takes unfair advantage of market rules to the detriment of other market participants and market efficiency.

For example, in 2013, the Commission found that JP Morgan violated the Anti-Manipulation Rule by engaging in twelve strategies over a two-year period in which it intentionally submitted bids to CAISO and MISO that falsely appeared economic to the market software, but were intended to, and in almost all cases did, lead CAISO and MISO to pay JP Morgan at rates far above market prices.[102] One example of such manipulative bidding is a gaming strategy in which JP Morgan submitted -$30/MWh day-ahead bids to CAISO for the end of day 1, and then the next day submitted energy bids of $999/MWh for the hours between midnight and 2 a.m. for day 2. CAISO's system evaluated only one day's bids at a time, and thus gave JP Morgan large day-ahead awards for the final hours of day 1. However, because CAISO's system also honors the physical limitations of power plants, the next day it gave JP Morgan ramp-down day-ahead awards for the first two hours of day 2. Those awards were priced at JP Morgan's $999/MWh bid price, even though market prices between midnight and 2 a.m. on day 2 were only about $12/MWh.[103]

Consistent with its previous findings on gaming, the Commission found that JP Morgan took unfair advantage of market rules by submitting bids not for the purpose of making money based on market fundamentals of supply and demand, "but to create artificial conditions that would cause the CAISO system to pay JP [Morgan] outside the market at premium rates."[104] The Commission also emphasized the harm that JP Morgan's bidding practices caused to the efficient operation of the CAISO and MISO markets.[105]

The Commission's recent decisions addressing the UTC investigations also concern prohibited gaming behavior. A UTC product is a type of spread trade that allows market participants to arbitrage the difference between day-ahead and real-time congestion prices at two different locations with no obligation to buy or sell physical power. In *Chen*, the Commission found that the respondents engaged in fraudulent UTC transactions in PJM markets solely to garner excessive credit payments that PJM paid to

---

"theoretical potential" for risk where evidence showed there was no "practical market risk").

[102] *JP Morgan*, 144 FERC ¶ 61,068 at P 4.

[103] *Id.* PP 57-68.

[104] *Id.* P 76.

[105] For example, the Commission noted the multiple CAISO and MISO Departments of Market Monitoring referrals to the Commission and multiple emergency tariff filings by CAISO or MISO that were prompted by JP Morgan's bidding practices. *JP Morgan*, 144 FERC ¶ 61,068 at PP 7–8, 78, 81.

transmission customers (known as MLSA payments).[106] In finding that the respondents engaged in a device, scheme, or artifice to defraud the PJM market, the Commission found that their round-trip UTC trades were like Enron's Death Star strategy in that they "involved offsetting pairs to capture revenues without providing the corresponding benefit to the market."[107] Additionally, the respondents' trades "falsely appeared to PJM as legitimate arbitrage-related trades when in fact they were nullities placed to garner MLSA payments" that otherwise would have been allocated to other market participants.[108] The Commission further found that the respondents' round-trip UTC trades were wash trades, and therefore *per se* fraudulent and manipulative.[109]

The Commission made similar findings in *City Power* and *Coaltrain*. In *City Power*, as it did in *Chen*, the Commission likened the respondents' round-trip UTC trades to Enron's Death Star strategy and found them to be wash trades.[110] In addition, in *City Power* and *Coaltrain*, the Commission identified two other types of UTC trades that were part of the manipulative scheme and the respondents' course of business to defraud, which involved either mathematically equivalent pricing nodes that experienced no price spreads,[111] or nodes that generated very small or negative price spreads that resulted in losses after accounting for the transaction costs associated with the trades, apart from the MLSA payments.[112] Although the respondents in *City Power* argued that their trades were not "gaming" because that term is too subjective and does not have a workable definition,[113] the Commission in all three UTC cases found the trades fraudulent given the totality of evidence presented and the respondents' purpose in making the trades.[114]

---

[106] *Chen*, 151 FERC ¶ 61,179 at PP 1–2.

[107] *Id.* P 64.

[108] *Id.* PP 69, 96.

[109] *Id.* P 102. The Commission further clarified in *Chen* that the market risk associated with a wash trade need not be zero—"it only need be small enough so that the risk has no practical or expected impact on the transaction." *Id.* P 104.

[110] *City Power*, 152 FERC ¶ 61,012 at PP 7, 126. Citing *Chen*, the Commission also found that the respondents' round-trip trades were contrary to the market design purposes for which PJM offered the UTC product. *Id.* P 100.

[111] *Id.* P 6; *Coaltrain*, 155 FERC ¶ 61,204 at P 118.

[112] *City Power*, 152 FERC ¶ 61,012 at PP 51-52; *Coaltrain*, 155 FERC ¶ 61,204 at PP 145, 147, 172.

[113] *City Power*, 152 FERC ¶ 61,012 at P 63.

[114] The Commission rejected similar arguments about "gaming" made by market participants in 2003 following the Western Energy Crisis. *See, e.g., Gaming Order*, 103 FERC ¶ 61,345 at PP 21, 23.

In doing so, the Commission found that the transactions at issue were made for the sole or primary purpose of targeting MLSA payments and not made to hedge or arbitrage—the market design purpose of UTC trades.[115] Given this purpose, the Commission found the trades to be deceptive because "they falsely appeared to PJM as being placed for the market design purpose of arbitraging price spreads."[116]

C. Misrepresentations

While cross-market manipulation and gaming are typically implemented through trading schemes, another category of conduct prohibited by the Commission's Anti-Manipulation Rule involves misrepresentations and omissions of material factual information.[117] This form of manipulation, like the cross-market and gaming schemes, dates back to the Western Energy Crisis when entities submitted false information to market operators and index publishers to take advantage of certain market rules and practices. In fact, the Commission incorporated language into the Anti-Manipulation Rule in response to the types of misrepresentations and omissions prevalent during the Western Energy Crisis. As stated in Order No. 670, "where an entity voluntarily provides information or where the entity is required by a tariff or a Commission statute, order, rule or regulation to provide information, and the entity then misrepresents or omits a material fact such that the information provided is materially misleading, there can be a violation of the Final Rule if all of the other elements of a violation are present."[118]

1. Pre-EPAct 2005 Misrepresentations and Omissions

During the Western Energy Crisis, one common type of misrepresentation involved the submission of false trade information to index publishers for the purpose of moving index prices to enhance the value of related positions tied to such prices. The index publishers, such as *Platts* and *Natural Gas Intelligence*, printed daily and monthly

---

[115] *Chen*, 151 FERC ¶ 61,179 at P 80; *City Power*, 152 FERC ¶ 61,012 at PP 103, 139, 158; *Coaltrain,* 155 FERC ¶ 61,204 at PP 5, 102, 104.

[116] *Chen*, 151 FERC ¶ 61,179 at PP 5, 96; *City Power*, 152 FERC ¶ 61,012 at PP 6, 126; *Coaltrain,* 155 FERC ¶ 61,204 at P 5.

[117] *See Maxim Power*, 151 FERC ¶ 61,094 at P 50 ("A violation of section 1c.2 may occur not only through a manipulative scheme, but through false statements and deceit."); *CES*, 144 FERC ¶ 61,163 at P 43, *Silkman*, 144 FERC ¶ 61,164 at P 43, and *Lincoln*, 144 FERC ¶ 61,162 at P 30 (determining that the Commission's Anti-Manipulation Rule includes "fraud's definition under the common law, i.e., any false statement, misrepresentation, or deceit").

[118] Order No. 670, FERC Stats. & Regs. ¶ 31,202 at P 41. This statement echoes language of the rule prohibiting entities from "mak[ing] any untrue statement of a material fact or . . . omit[ting] to state a material fact . . . ." 18 C.F.R. Part 1c (2016).

index prices based on the volume-weighted average price of reported trades. To improperly influence the index prices, many market participants simply reported lies, which included "fabricating trades, inflating the volume of trades, omitting trades, and adjusting the price of trades."[119] For example, in 2002, Dynegy entered into a $5 million settlement with the CFTC for "report[ing] false natural gas trading information, including price and volume information, to certain reporting firms."[120] It did this "in an attempt to skew . . . indexes to [its] financial benefit."[121] In another example of misrepresentations during the Western Energy Crisis, entities engaged in selling "Phantom Ancillary Services" in the CAISO market, dubbed "Get Shorty" by Enron and other market participants and discussed *supra* at section IV.B.1.[122]

2. Post-EPAct 2005 Misrepresentations and Omissions

Market participants have continued to harm energy markets through misrepresentations and omissions in the post-EPAct 2005 environment. To combat this practice, the Commission has used its anti-manipulation authority to hold entities accountable. In doing so, the Commission has provided guidance on the types of misrepresentations and omissions that violate the Anti-Manipulation Rule and the harm that stems from these violations. For example, in a group of four cases involving ISO-NE's Day-Ahead Load Response Program (DALRP), the Commission found that two entities misrepresented their typical load and their ability to reduce load by adjusting their energy use during an initial "baseline" period.[123] Specifically, under the DALRP, ISO-NE compensated customers for load reductions, as measured against a baseline load amount established during a five-day period that was supposed to represent the company's normal electricity usage.[124] The Commission found that two paper mills in Maine misrepresented to ISO-NE that they had a higher load amount when they intentionally reduced their on-site generation and purchased more power from the grid

---

[119] *Final Report on Price Manipulation in Western Markets*, at ES-6.

[120] *In re Dynegy Mktg. & Trade & West Coast Power LLC*, CFTC Docket No. 03-03, at *1.

[121] *Id*; *see also In re El Paso Merchant Energy, L.P.*, CFTC Docket No. 03-09, at *2 ($20 million settlement with CFTC for misreporting trade information and withholding information about actual trades).

[122] *San Diego Gas & Elec. Co.*, 149 FERC ¶ 61,116 at P 186 n.414.

[123] *See Rumford Paper Co.*, 142 FERC ¶ 61,218 (2013) (settlement); *CES*, 144 FERC ¶ 61,163 (order assessing civil penalty); *Silkman*, 144 FERC ¶ 61,164 (order assessing civil penalty); *Lincoln*, 144 FERC ¶ 61,162 (order assessing civil penalty); *Lincoln Paper and Tissue, LLC*, 155 FERC ¶ 61,228 (2016) (settlement).

[124] *CES*, 144 FERC ¶ 61,163 at P 11; *Silkman*, 144 FERC ¶ 61,164 at P 11; *Lincoln*, 144 FERC ¶ 61,162 at P 12.

during the five-day baseline period.[125] Then, after the baseline period, the mills resumed normal use of their on-site generation and purchased less energy from the grid, thus creating the illusion that they had reduced electricity consumption.[126] As a result, the mills received DALRP payments from ISO-NE that were for nonexistent demand response reductions. The mills' misrepresentations resulted in ISO-NE paying millions of dollars (on behalf of its customers) for what amounted to phantom load reductions.[127]

Similar to the behavior in DALRP, the Commission found in *Enerwise Global Technologies, Inc.* that a demand response aggregator had misrepresented a demand response customer's potential load reduction capability by basing the potential reduction quantity on the simultaneous operation of two backup generators when reliable operation of both generators in parallel with the grid was not possible.[128] Enerwise also engaged in misrepresentations to the RTO by instructing its customer to inflate its electricity consumption baseline prior to certain events to make the supposed reduction in electricity consumption appear larger than it actually was.[129]

---

[125] *CES*, 144 FERC ¶ 61,163 at P 43; *Lincoln*, 144 FERC ¶ 61,162 at P 30.

[126] In DALRP, the Commission considered the respondents' departure from their prior practices as an indicium of fraud. *See CES*, 144 FERC ¶ 61,163 at P 49 (holding that the paper mill's departure from routine use of on-site generation, among other factors, "demonstrates . . . fraudulent actions"); *Silkman*, 144 FERC ¶ 61,164 at P 43; *Lincoln*, 144 FERC ¶ 61,162 at P 30. A departure from prior practices does not necessarily indicate a fraudulent motive, but, combined with other factors and absent legitimate explanations for the difference, can create a reasonable inference of fraud. The Commission has also considered this potential indicium in cross-market manipulations. *See Barclays*, 144 FERC ¶ 61,041 at P 32 (considering "the difference in Respondents' trading behavior in the Manipulation Months from those months where manipulation was not alleged"); *Deutsche Bank*, 142 FERC ¶ 61,056 at P 3 (noting that traders had not done any physical trading "until they undertook the physical trades at issue in this matter"); *MISO Virtual & FTR Trading*, 146 FERC ¶ 61,072 at P 4 (noting differences in company's FTR positions and virtual trading between manipulation and non-manipulation periods).

[127] *CES*, 144 FERC ¶ 61,163 at P 90 and *Silkman*, 144 FERC ¶ 61,164 at P 84 (finding that ISO-NE paid more than $3 million for non-existent demand response reductions across a six month period attributable to the Rumford paper mill's artificially inflated baseline); *see also Lincoln*, 144 FERC ¶ 61,162 at P 68 (finding that ISO-NE paid more than $445,000 for non-existent demand response reductions across a six-month period attributable to the Lincoln paper mill's artificially inflated baseline).

[128] *Enerwise Global Techs., Inc.*, 143 FERC ¶ 61,218, at P 6 (2013).

[129] *Id.*

30

Other misrepresentations have involved false statements or omissions regarding basic factual information. For example, the Commission found in *Maxim Power* that the company falsely represented in its energy offers and statements to the independent market monitor (IMM) that it was running its generator on high-price fuel oil when in fact it was burning cheaper natural gas.[130] The Commission found that Maxim did this in an attempt to obtain payments from the ISO "based on burning oil that were substantially higher than if its payments were based on using natural gas."[131] Maxim's misrepresentations included its offers that were based on oil prices, as well as misleading statements to the market monitor that pipeline flow restrictions prevented Maxim from obtaining natural gas.[132] Maxim also failed to tell the market monitor that it had been burning natural gas after it submitted offers based on oil prices.[133] The Commission found that Maxim's "careful omission of this information, which was essential to protecting Maxim's significant profits, was not accidental."[134] The Commission held that "[t]hese statements and omissions were intended to impede the IMM's review of Maxim's behavior and hampered the IMM's ability to mitigate Maxim's offers."[135]

Another example of a factual misrepresentation violating the Anti-Manipulation Rule is the 2011 Commission settlement with Holyoke Gas and Electric Department, in which Holyoke admitted that it neither notified ISO-NE of three planned outages nor scheduled them consistent with the ISO's tariff requirements.[136] Holyoke also stipulated that it offered the out-of-service units' energy into the market, despite knowing that they could not have provided the energy if dispatched.[137] Holyoke committed fraud on the market by accepting more than $300,000 in capacity payments for out-of-service resources.[138]

In another case involving a misrepresentation of basic factual information, Gila River falsely labeled transactions in CAISO to avoid congestion impacts at the Palo Verde intertie.[139] Gila River preferred to sell power at Palo Verde because of low

---

[130] *Maxim Power*, 151 FERC ¶ 61,094 at PP 3–4.

[131] *Id.* P 49.

[132] *Id.*

[133] *Id.*

[134] *Id.* P 91.

[135] *Id.* P 49.

[136] *In re Holyoke Gas & Elec. Dep't*, 137 FERC ¶ 61,159, at P 3 (2011).

[137] *Id.*

[138] *Id.* P 10.

[139] *Gila River*, 141 FERC ¶ 61,136.

transmission costs, but congestion at that point limited the amount of imports there.[140] The CAISO tariff allowed entities with a resource and load outside of CAISO to avoid congestion impacts by designating their transactions as "Wheeling-Through," indicating that power was wheeled through California from a linked import point to a linked export point.[141] Despite the fact that Gila River's transactions did not meet CAISO's definition of "Wheeling-Through" because they lacked a resource and load outside of CAISO, it falsely designated its transactions as Wheeling-Through, thus allowing it to continue selling power at Palo Verde without being negatively impacted by congestion there.[142] This action "undermined the proper functioning of the CAISO market."[143]

More recently, in a 2016 Commission settlement involving misrepresentations and omissions, Berkshire Power Company LLC (Berkshire Power) and Power Plant Management Services LLC (PPMS) admitted that Berkshire Power engaged in a fraudulent scheme, directed by the Projects General Manager, to perform unreported maintenance work and to conceal that work and associated maintenance outages from ISO-NE.[144] The companies acknowledged that individuals at the natural gas-fired plant scheduled maintenance work for times when the plant was unlikely to be dispatched and then failed to notify ISO-NE about the work or the plant's associated unavailability at least sixteen times during a period just over three years.[145] And there were at least six instances in which employees falsely represented to ISO-NE dispatchers that the plant was starting up or able to start up when, in fact, the plant was unavailable due to ongoing maintenance or technical problems.[146]

V.   Mitigating and Aggravating Factors Relevant to Market Manipulation

In various policy statements and in its Penalty Guidelines, the Commission has described the various mitigating and aggravating factors affecting penalties for violations of its rules, including the Anti-Manipulation Rule.[147] The Commission has also provided

---

[140] *Id.* P 3.

[141] *Id.* P 5.

[142] *Id.* PP 5, 12–13.

[143] *Id.* P 15.

[144] *Berkshire Power Co. LLC & Power Plant Mgmt. Servs. LLC*, 154 FERC ¶ 61,259, at P 8 (2016) (*Berkshire Power*).

[145] *Id.*

[146] *Id.* P 11.

[147] *See, e.g.*, *Enforcement of Statutes, Orders, Rules, and Regulations*, 113 FERC ¶ 61,068, at PP 21–27 (2005) (2005 Policy Statement on Enforcement); *Enforcement of Statutes, Regulations, and Orders*, 123 FERC ¶ 61,156, at PP 55–71 (2008) (Revised

valuable notice on mitigating and aggravating factors in its orders approving settlement agreements and orders assessing civil penalties in specific market manipulation matters. These factors, which are relevant to the Commission's statutory mandate to consider the seriousness of violations and efforts to remedy them, include entities' commitment to compliance, self-reporting, cooperation, prior history of violations, involvement of senior-level employees, obstructionist conduct, and acceptance of responsibility.

This section focuses on three such factors—commitment to compliance, self-reporting, and cooperation—which have played a significant role in shaping penalty determinations in multiple market manipulation cases. These factors can have a substantial impact on the applicable penalty range under the Penalty Guidelines as well as where within the range the Commission determines to set the ultimate penalty. Entities have control over each of these factors and can take steps before violations occur, when they occur, or after the commencement of an investigation to lessen their culpability and resulting penalty.

A. Commitment to Compliance

The Commission has consistently emphasized the importance of compliance in its enforcement program. In fact, on the first page of its Penalty Guidelines, the Commission highlights that "[a]chieving compliance, not assessing penalties, is the central goal of the Commission's enforcement efforts."[148] True to this policy objective, the Commission provides substantial penalty reductions to entities that have effective compliance programs and has outlined certain factors that are helpful in achieving effective compliance.

Under the Penalty Guidelines, entities can receive up to a three-point credit to reduce their culpability score for an effective compliance program.[149] This reduction is substantial. As the Commission explained when issuing the Penalty Guidelines, "even if an organization fails to receive any reduction other than compliance credit, the compliance credit alone could still reduce a penalty by sixty percent, for example, from $5 million to $2 million."[150] Conversely, the Commission has made clear that a lack of

---

Policy Statement on Enforcement); *Compliance with Statutes, Regulations, and Orders,* 125 FERC ¶ 61,058, at PP 13–21 (2008) (Policy Statement on Compliance); *Enforcement of Statutes, Orders, Rules, and Regulations,* 132 FERC ¶ 61,216 (2010) (Revised Policy Statement on Penalty Guidelines attaching the FERC Penalty Guidelines).

[148] FERC Penalty Guidelines § 1A1.1.2.

[149] *Id.* § 1C2.3(f).

[150] Revised Policy Statement on Penalty Guidelines, 132 FERC ¶ 61,216 at P 109. The Commission has also stated that, when combined with other elements, the compliance credit can even eliminate civil penalties. Policy Statement on Compliance, 125 FERC ¶ 61,058 at P 23.

compliance can aggravate a penalty determination, explaining that it could "assess a penalty that falls on the higher side of the penalty range" or "depart from applying the Penalty Guidelines" in cases when an entity lacks effective compliance.[151]

The Commission has given entities the opportunity to obtain compliance credit by outlining the factors relevant to effective compliance. The Penalty Guidelines devote an entire chapter to compliance, detailing seven factors required for an effective compliance program.[152] These factors, which are consistent with the Commission's previous policy statements, include, among others, establishing standards and procedures to prevent and detect violations, taking reasonable steps to respond appropriately after a violation has been detected, and periodically evaluating the effectiveness of the organization's compliance program.[153]

The Commission often grants compliance credit in its market manipulation matters, with the 2014 *Direct Energy* case providing a notable example of the ability of effective compliance to significantly reduce a company's civil penalties.[154] In *Direct Energy*, staff found that traders had engaged in a cross-market manipulation scheme by making fixed-price trades designed to suppress the *Gas Daily* index to benefit their related financial positions.[155] In approving a $20,000 civil penalty—a low penalty for a market manipulation violation—the Commission emphasized Direct Energy's robust compliance program, including the program's effectiveness in promptly detecting and responding to the violations. Direct Energy caught the violations through two independent means: (1) a trader reported them after receiving training on the Commission's *Constellation* settlement; and (2) the company's back office flagged the trades as unusually large.[156] After discovering the violations, Direct Energy took appropriate steps to self-report, investigate, and discipline the traders. All of these findings factored into the finding of an effective compliance program and the resultant substantial penalty credit.[157] Also important, Direct Energy's compliance program, by detecting and stopping the relevant conduct early, substantially reduced the market harm

---

[151] Revised Policy Statement on Penalty Guidelines, 132 FERC ¶ 61,216 at P 131.

[152] *See* FERC Penalty Guidelines § 1B2.1.

[153] *See id.*

[154] *Direct Energy*, 148 FERC ¶ 61,114.

[155] *Id.* P 15.

[156] *Id.* PP 4–5.

[157] *Id.* PP 12, 20.

from the manipulative conduct that would have continued into the future if left undetected.[158]

Companies should use the *Direct Energy* case as a guide when building an effective compliance program. Direct Energy's compliance plan was more than just a written document; it was a program, supported and followed at all levels of the organization, that worked in practice to detect, cease, and respond to violations quickly and effectively. In contrast, the Commission has refused to provide any compliance credit to some entities that had documented compliance programs but did not follow them.[159]

B. Self-Reporting

The Commission "place[s] great importance on self-reporting" because of the "significant value [it adds] to overall industry compliance."[160] The Commission explains this value as follows: "Providing credit for self-reporting gives organizations an incentive to detect and correct violations early. Self-reporting also assists the Commission's review of violations and facilitates the process of providing remedies to

---

[158] As with any violation, the impact of a robust compliance program on potential penalties depends on the interaction with a number of other factors as discussed in the Penalty Guidelines, and staff will continue to consider and recommend settlements or penalties to the Commission on a case-by-case basis.

[159] *See, e.g.*, *Deutsche Bank*, 142 FERC ¶ 61,056 at P 25 (company's compliance handbook discussed the type of trading at issue, but the trading was nonetheless not reviewed by management); *Barclays*, 144 FERC ¶ 61,041 at P 123 (ineffective compliance program); *Constellation*, 138 FERC ¶ 61,168 at P 27 (same); *City Power*, 152 FERC ¶ 61,012 at P 248 (compliance credit not warranted even if it had a program in place "given that City Power's founder and majority owner designed and directed the fraudulent trading conduct"); *EnerNOC, Inc. & Celerity Energy Partners San Diego LLC*, 141 FERC ¶ 61,211, at P 13 (2012) (order approving settlement finding that Celerity, which failed to comply with certain Commission filing requirements, had no compliance procedures regarding regulatory filing obligations); *Berkshire Power*, 154 FERC ¶ 61,259 at P 21 (order approving settlement in which neither company had an effective compliance program in place); *BP*, 156 FERC ¶ 61,031 at PP 397-398, 402 (agreeing with ALJ's findings that BP's compliance program was deficient in operation, in part, because it was not consistently followed).

[160] Revised Policy Statement on Penalty Guidelines, 132 FERC ¶ 61,216 at P 141. In the 2015 fiscal year, staff closed 78 self-reports from that and prior years with no action. FERC Office of Enforcement, 2015 Report on Enforcement, Docket No. AD07-13-009, at 15 (2015), *available at* http://www.ferc.gov/legal/staff-reports/2015/11-19-15-enforcement.pdf. (2015 Report on Enforcement).

affected parties."[161] Because of this value, the Commission provides a two-point self-reporting credit under the Penalty Guidelines, which, alone, can result in a forty percent reduction in base penalty amount.[162]

The Commission has also described what it expects of entities in order to secure the full two-point credit. To receive credit, the Commission requires prompt disclosures of potential violations about which it would otherwise not be aware.[163] Thus, the Commission provides self-reporting credit for disclosures made "(A) prior to an imminent threat of disclosure or government investigation; and (B) within a reasonably prompt time after becoming aware of the violation."[164]

Direct Energy again provides a good example of self-reporting that warranted and received full credit under the Penalty Guidelines. In May 2012, very soon after discovering potential violations, Direct Energy contacted staff to make an initial, verbal self-report. Counsel proposed to conduct an internal investigation and then submit a written self-report. After assessing the circumstances, staff agreed to this proposal. Counsel periodically updated staff on the company's internal investigation and, in August 2012, met with staff to describe the results of the investigation and submit a written self-report.[165] A number of other companies have taken this useful and effective approach to self-reporting (and addressing) potential violations.

In contrast to Direct Energy's approach, some companies might opt not to make a prompt self-report of market manipulation, deciding instead to wait until they are certain a violation occurred. Or, they might decide to forego market manipulation-related self-reports altogether, reasoning that there is too much risk of external exposure from market manipulation findings. However, companies should consider a few factors before making such decisions. First, there is real value in *prompt* self-reports, and entities may lose full self-reporting credit if they delay too long.[166] Prompt self-reports, for example,

---

[161] Revised Policy Statement on Penalty Guidelines, 132 FERC ¶ 61,216 at P 141. In 2005, the Commission explained that "[c]ompanies are in the best position to detect and correct violations of our orders, rules, and regulations, both inadvertent and intentional, and should be proactive in doing so." 2005 Policy Statement on Enforcement, 113 FERC ¶ 61,068 at P 24.

[162] FERC Penalty Guidelines § 1C2.3(g)(1).

[163] *Id.*; *see also* Revised Policy Statement on Enforcement, 123 FERC ¶ 61,156 at PP 61-64.

[164] FERC Penalty Guidelines § 1C2.3(g)(1).

[165] *Direct Energy*, 148 FERC ¶ 61,114 at P 3.

[166] In fact, a long delay could result in the lack of any credit if, for example, staff discovers the potential violations through other sources, such as from a whistleblower.

allow staff to provide guidance and directives to reporting entities on factors to consider in their internal investigations. Second, submitting a self-report does not necessarily mean that staff will open an investigation. Each matter, whether self-reported or not, is assessed on its own merits, and many matters are not opened. Even if staff does open an investigation, it may or may not lead to a finding of violations and subsequent sanctions. Finally, a self-report does not amount to an admission of a market manipulation violation (or any violation).[167]

C. Cooperation

The Commission also places great importance on good-faith and consistent cooperation throughout an investigation because that "help[s] provide Enforcement staff with sufficient information to understand the circumstances of how and why the violation occurred as well as the identity of the relevant personnel involved in the violation."[168] "As is the case with good-faith self-reports, this type of cooperation should lead to a better informed and prompt conclusion of staff's inquiry."[169] Therefore, the Commission provides a one-point credit for cooperation to reduce a company's culpability score and has provided extensive guidance on what is required to achieve this credit. To receive the credit, the cooperation must be timely and thorough, meaning that it begins at the time an entity is notified of an investigation and results in the disclosure of information "sufficient for the Commission to identify the nature and extent of the violation and the individual(s) responsible for the violation."[170]

There are positive examples of timely and thorough cooperation in market manipulation investigations, and also examples where the failure to cooperate was an important factor in the Commission's penalty determination. Most entities cooperate with staff's investigative efforts by timely producing pertinent information and witnesses.[171] For example in *Gila River,* the Commission found that "Gila River and its

---

[167] *See, e.g., Direct Energy,* 148 FERC ¶ 61,114 at P 2 (neither admitting nor denying violations after making a good-faith, prompt self-report). If an entity does admit to a violation, however, that can reduce its civil penalty under the Penalty Guidelines. *See, e.g., MISO Cinergy Hub Transactions,* 149 FERC ¶ 61,278 at PP 2, 11 (receiving credit for admitting to market manipulation violations); *Gila River,* 141 FERC ¶ 61,136 at P 1 (receiving credit for admitting to market manipulation violations).

[168] Revised Policy Statement on Penalty Guidelines, 132 FERC ¶ 61,216 at P 142.

[169] *Id.*

[170] FERC Penalty Guidelines § 1C2.3(g), Application Note 11.

[171] Of course, to receive cooperation credit the production of information and witnesses must also be in good faith. For example, cooperation credit would not be warranted for producing a witness that is coached to be uncooperative or to provide false or misleading testimony.

employees provided exemplary cooperation in the investigation and were productive and diligent in assisting staff at all phases of its investigation. Further, Gila River's cooperation made staff's fact-finding efficient and productive and thereby helped conserve Commission resources."[172] As discussed in the settlement agreement in that matter, Enforcement found that "[t]ogether with its attorneys, Gila River employees worked with Enforcement staff to bring to light salient facts and to develop a sound method to analyze and calculate Gila River's profits from its conduct. In agreeing to a penalty amount, Enforcement favorably considered this conduct of Gila River and its employees."[173]

In stark contrast, the Commission recently denied mitigating credit for cooperation in *City Power*, finding that the company and individual trader made "very serious" intentional misrepresentations to staff about the existence of relevant instant messages. The Commission considered such misrepresentations as obstructionist conduct and an aggravating factor in its penalty calculations.[174] Similarly, the Commission denied cooperation credit in *Coaltrain* based on the company's "fail[ure] to acknowledge the existence of or produce" relevant data to staff.[175] In another example of a failure to earn cooperation credit, the Commission considered in *Lincoln* the respondent's failure to supplement investigatory data requests regarding its financial condition and its subsequent submission of different financial information directly to the Commission as part of the Order to Show Cause proceeding.[176] The respondent had also delayed production of a number of emails requested by staff and only agreed to provide those emails in a usable format after multiple requests.[177] Finding the respondent's cooperation was neither timely nor thorough, the Commission denied cooperation credit in assessing

---

[172] *Gila River*, 141 FERC ¶ 61,136 at P 16.

[173] *Gila River*, 141 FERC ¶ 61,136, Settlement Agreement at P 3.

[174] *City Power*, 152 FERC ¶ 61,012 at PP 241–47 ("These violations caused OE Staff to waste valuable time and resources during their investigative process."); *see also* *JP Morgan*, 144 FERC ¶ 61,068 at P 89 ("[I]n light of the record here, we remind all persons under investigation of the importance of candor and accuracy during all stages of Market Monitor inquiries and Commission investigations.").

[175] *Coaltrain,* 155 FERC ¶ 61,204 at P 324.

[176] *Lincoln*, 144 FERC ¶ 61,162 at P 74.

[177] *Id.*

penalties.[178] The failure to cooperate, as highlighted in these cases, impedes staff's ability to investigate and resolve matters timely and efficiently.[179]

VI.   Staff Decisions to Close Investigations of Allegations of Market Manipulation

While the Commission's settlements, orders to show cause, orders assessing civil penalties, and staff notices of alleged violation often receive the most public attention, staff closes a significant number of its market manipulation investigations with no action after finding no violation.

Staff's publicly available Annual Reports on Enforcement provide illustrative examples of market manipulation investigations that were opened but later closed.[180] Staff also provides its reasons for closing the investigations. Like the Commission's guidance on what constitutes manipulation, describing conduct that does *not* warrant penalties provides useful notice and guidance to industry. It provides valuable information to market participants, for example, on developing effective preventative and mitigation measures.

As an example from staff's Annual Report on Enforcement in fiscal year 2015, staff investigated whether a financial trading firm had engaged in cross-market manipulation on one day in 2014 by submitting virtual bids with the intent to benefit its existing FTR position.[181] The bids themselves lost money, and they caused the value of the firm's FTR position to increase substantially. After requesting documents and taking testimony of the relevant trader, staff found insufficient evidence of manipulative intent. In particular, the trader provided a credible, legitimate explanation for his decision to place those virtual trades, and the company produced an email from the trader to his supervisor, noting that his virtual trades might have affected the company's FTR position and explaining that this result was unexpected and that he would cease trading at those

---

[178] *Id.*

[179] *See, e.g., Coaltrain,* 155 FERC ¶ 61,204 at P 317; *In Re Edison Mission,* 123 FERC ¶ 61, 170, at P 9 (2008) (considering that Edison Mission's "acts that misled staff were protracted, related to core issues under investigation, and caused extensive misallocation of resources"). The Commission places great emphasis on cooperation to avoid such waste and delay during investigations. Revised Policy Statement on Penalty Guidelines, 132 FERC ¶ 61,216 at P 142 (explaining that good-faith, consistent, and continuing cooperation "should lead to a better informed and prompt conclusion of staff's inquiry").

[180] *See, e.g.,* FERC Office of Enforcement, 2016 Report on Enforcement, Docket No. AD07-13-010, at 31-32 (2016) (issued simultaneously with this White Paper and available on the Commission's website).

[181] 2015 Report on Enforcement at 30.

nodes in the future. Based on insufficient evidence of manipulative intent, the limited duration of the trading, the fact that the RTO/ISO might have been able to claw back any gains realized through these trades, and discussions with the company in which it identified new protective measures that it had taken to avoid problems with virtual trades in the future, staff closed this investigation without further action.[182]

As discussed in the same annual report, staff also investigated whether a demand response aggregator had violated the Anti-Manipulation Rule and the relevant RTO/ISO tariff by enrolling a resource in a yearly demand response capacity program while knowing the resource's operating level could potentially vary widely during the delivery year.[183] After taking testimony and reviewing written discovery, staff determined that although the aggregator received information regarding potential variations in the resource's operating level before enrollment, it lacked sufficient details regarding the timing and extent of potential changes in the resource's operating level to draw conclusions regarding its participation. In addition, staff found no evidence that the aggregator enrolled the resource intending to take advantage of potential changes in its operating level and closed the investigation after considering these factors.[184]

An example from staff's 2014 Report on Enforcement is an investigation where staff examined whether a financial institution engaged in manipulation by increasing the quantities of CRRs held at two locations and proceeding to schedule price-taking physical import bids at one of the locations.[185] Staff investigated whether those physical imports were part of an effort to exacerbate congestion at the intertie location to increase the value of the CRR position. After determining that the groups responsible for the CRRs and imports operated independently and that economic fundamentals supported the behavior, staff closed the investigation.[186] In another example from the 2014 report, staff investigated an entity based on internal information showing a potential cross-market manipulation scheme at two California natural gas trading hubs.[187] The entity was engaging in unusually large physical transactions and initially failed to provide consistent explanations for its conduct.[188] After reviewing the relevant trade data and interviewing

---

[182] *Id.*

[183] *Id.* at 29.

[184] *Id.*

[185] FERC Office of Enforcement, 2014 Report on Enforcement, Docket No. AD07-13-008, at 27 (2014), *available at* http://www.ferc.gov/legal/staff-reports/2014/11-20-14-enforcement.pdf.

[186] *Id.*

[187] *Id.*

[188] *Id.*

the relevant traders, staff closed the matter because the facts showed legitimate trading activity and did not indicate intent to benefit the entity's financial positions.[189]

In another example from staff's 2013 Report on Enforcement, a financial institution self-reported that it discovered an instant message between two of its traders potentially indicating the intentional use of virtual bidding to affect locational marginal prices in an RTO/ISO and thereby influence the value of related financial positions.[190] After analyzing company trades and documents and taking testimony, staff determined there was insufficient evidence of a manipulative trading scheme. Staff also found that the company self-reported the matter promptly and took immediate remedial steps and that the matter involved an isolated trading period. Because of all of these factors, staff closed the investigation with no action.[191] Finally, in an example from staff's 2012 Report on Enforcement, staff investigated allegations that a market participant in an organized electric market engaged in manipulation by executing virtual transactions at or near nodes where it owned financial transmission rights for the purpose of artificially inflating the value of those rights.[192] Staff closed the investigation because there was insufficient evidence to prove that the virtual transactions were aimed at manipulating prices.[193]

VII.   Conclusion

As described in this White Paper, since EPAct 2005 and the implementation of the Anti-Manipulation Rule, the Commission has taken significant steps to carry out its statutory obligation to effectively and vigorously police and sanction manipulative conduct. This is reflected in the number of market manipulation settlements and enforcement proceedings the Commission has pursued and approved, the civil penalties and disgorgement the Commission has imposed to deter and remedy manipulative conduct, and the compliance program enhancements the Commission has required entities to adopt to help avoid future instances of manipulation. In addition, the Commission has become more proactive in its efforts to detect manipulation, most significantly, by creating the Division of Analytics and Surveillance to conduct complex

---

[189] *Id.*

[190] FERC Office of Enforcement, 2013 Report on Enforcement, Docket No. AD07-13-006, at 26 (2013), *available at* http://www.ferc.gov/legal/staff-reports/2013/11-21-13-enforcement.pdf.

[191] *Id.*

[192] FERC Office of Enforcement, 2012 Report on Enforcement, Docket No. AD07-13-005, at 23 (2012), *available at* http://www.ferc.gov/legal/staff-reports/11-15-12-enforcement.pdf.

[193] *Id.*

forensic analyses of market data to determine whether manipulation is occurring. This is the type of strong enforcement program Congress expected when passing EPAct 2005. Indeed, in the aftermath of the Western Energy Crisis, the Senate Governmental Affairs Committee told then-Chairman Patrick Wood III that "[m]embers of both parties on the Committee [share the interest] that FERC learn . . . from the Enron scandal and . . . [be] as aggressive and sophisticated as the players out in the deregulated energy market. "[194]

The Commission has worked vigorously to detect, pursue, and sanction market manipulation while ensuring a fair and thorough enforcement process.[195] And the Commission has also sought to be as transparent as reasonably possible (while always looking for opportunities to be more transparent) in providing guidance to market participants about what conduct constitutes market manipulation and what conduct does not.

---

[194] *Asleep at the Switch: FERC's Oversight of the Enron Corporation: Hearing Before the S. Comm. on Gov't Affairs*, 107th Cong. 59 (2003) (statement of Sen. Joseph Lieberman, Chairman, S. Comm. on Governmental Affairs).

[195] 2005 Policy Statement on Enforcement, 113 FERC ¶ 61,068 at P 1; *see also* Todd Hettenbach, Allison Murphy & Thomas Olson, *The FERC Enforcement Process*, 35 Energy L. J. 283, 291-97 (2014); *Hearing on Discussion Draft on Accountability and Dep't of Energy Perspectives on Title IV: Energy Efficiency Before the H. Energy and Commerce Comm. Energy and Power Subcomm*, 114th Cong. 34-37 (2015) (statement of Larry R. Parkinson, Director, FERC Office of Enforcement).

APPENDIX A

Market Manipulation Matters Post-Anti-Manipulation Rule

Commission-Approved Settlements:

- *In re Amaranth Advisors*, 128 FERC ¶ 61,154 (2009)
- *In re Jefferson Energy Trading, LLC*, 126 FERC ¶ 61,040 (2009)
- *In re Klabzuba Oil & Gas, F.L.P.*, 126 FERC ¶ 61,040 (2009)
- *In re ONEOK, Inc.*, 126 FERC ¶ 61,040 (2009)
- *In re Tenaska Mktg. Ventures*, 126 FERC ¶ 61,040 (2009)
- *N. Am. Power Partners*, 133 FERC ¶ 61,089 (2010)
- *In re Atmos Energy Corp.*, 137 FERC ¶ 61,190 (2011)
- *In re Holyoke Gas & Elec. Dept.*, 137 FERC ¶ 61,159 (2011)
- *Gila River Power, LLC*, 141 FERC ¶ 61,136 (2012)
- *Constellation Energy Commodities Grp., Inc.*, 138 FERC ¶ 61,168 (2012)
- *In re Joseph Polidoro*, 138 FERC ¶ 61,018 (2012)
- *In re Make-Whole Payments & Related Bidding Strategies*, 144 FERC ¶ 61,068 (2013)
- *Enerwise Global Technologies, Inc.*, 143 FERC ¶ 61,218 (2013)
- *Rumford Paper Co.*, 142 FERC ¶ 61,218 (2013)
- *In re PJM Up-To Congestion Transactions.*, 142 FERC ¶ 61,088 (2013)
- *Deutsche Bank Energy Trading, LLC*, 142 FERC ¶ 61,056 (2013)
- *MISO Cinergy Hub Transactions*, 149 FERC ¶ 61,278 (2014)
- *Direct Energy Servs., Inc.*, 148 FERC ¶ 61,114 (2014)
- *MISO Virtual & FTR Trading*, 146 FERC ¶ 61,072 (2014)
- *Berkshire Power Co. LLC & Power Plant Mgmt. Servs. LLC*, 154 FERC ¶ 61,259 (2016)
- *Lincoln Paper and Tissue, LLC*, 155 FERC ¶ 61,228 (2016)
- *National Energy & Trade, L.P.*, 156 FERC ¶ 61,154 (2016)
- *In re David Silva*, 156 FERC ¶ 61,155 (2016)
- *Maxim Power Corp.*, 156 FERC ¶ 61,223 (2016)

Matters Tried in Administrative Proceedings:

- *Brian Hunter*, 135 FERC ¶ 61,054 (2011), *order denying reh'g*, 137 FERC ¶ 61,146 (2011), *rev'd sub nom*, *Hunter v. FERC*, 711 F.3d 155 (D.C. Cir. 2013)
- *BP America, Inc.*, 156 FERC ¶ 61,031 (2016) (Order on Initial Decision and Rehearing)

Commission Orders Assessing Civil Penalties

- *Lincoln Paper & Tissue, LLC*, 144 FERC ¶ 61,162 (2013)

- *Silkman, LLC*, 144 FERC ¶ 61,164 (2013)
- *Competitive Energy Servs., LLC*, 144 FERC ¶ 61,163 (2013)
- *Barclays Bank, PLC*, 144 FERC ¶ 61,041 (2013)
- *Maxim Power Corp.*, 151 FERC ¶ 61,094 (2015)
- *Houlian Chen*, 151 FERC ¶ 61,179 (2015)
- *City Power Mktg., LLC*, 152 FERC ¶ 61,012 (2015)
- *Coaltrain Energy, L.P.*, 155 FERC ¶ 61,204 (2016)
- *ETRACOM & Michael Rosenberg*, 155 FERC ¶ 61,284 (2016)

District Court Proceedings on Petition to Affirm Penalty Assessments:

- *FERC v. Barclays Bank, PLC*, No. 2:13-cv-2093-TLA-EFB (TEMP) (E.D. Cal.)
- *FERC v. Silkman and Competitive Energy Servs., LLC*, No. 1:13-cv-13054 (D. Me.)
- *FERC v. Lincoln Paper & Tissue, LLC*, No. 1:13-cv-13056 (D. Me.) (Settled on June 1, 2016)
- *FERC v. Maxim Power Corp.*, No. 3:15-cv-30113 (D. Mass.) (Settled on Sept. 26, 2016)
- *FERC v. City Power Mktg., LLC*, No. 1:15-cv-01428-JDB (D.D.C.)
- *FERC v. Powhatan Energy Fund, LLC*, No. 3:15-cv-0452 (E.D. Va.)
- *FERC v. ETRACOM LLC*, No. 2:16-at-01011 (E.D. Cal.)
- *FERC v. Coaltrain Energy, L.P.*, No. 2:16-cv-732 (S.D. Ohio)

Pending Order to Show Cause (OSC) Proceedings at the Commission:

- *Total Gas & Power N. Am.*, 155 FERC ¶ 61,105 (2016) (OSC and Notice of Proposed Penalty)
- *BP America, Inc.*, 156 FERC ¶ 61,031 (2016) (Order on Initial Decision and Rehearing)